THE COMPLETE
QUICK &
HEARTY

Diabetic Cookbook

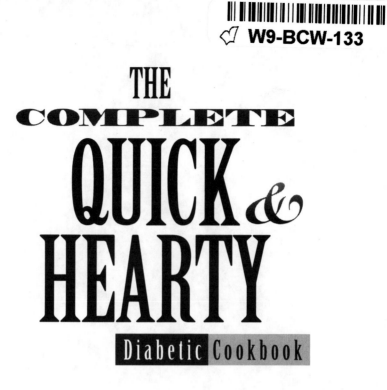

THE COMPLETE

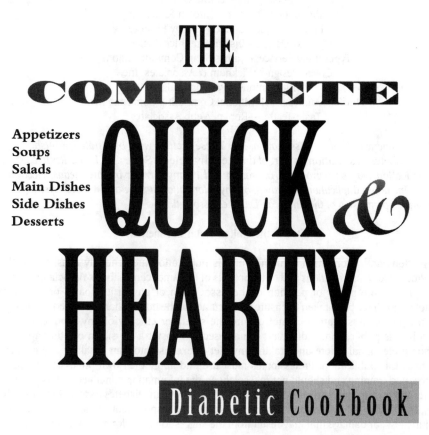

Appetizers
Soups
Salads
Main Dishes
Side Dishes
Desserts

QUICK & HEARTY

Diabetic Cookbook

More than 250 fast,
low-fat recipes
with old-fashioned
good taste

American
Diabetes
Association®

Book Editor—Laurie Guffey
Production Director—Carolyn R. Segree
Production Coordinator—Peggy M. Rote
Text Design—Insight Graphics, Inc.
Typesetting Services—James Stein Communications
Cover Design—Wickham & Associates, Inc.
Illustrations—Patricia Walsh
Nutrient Analysis—Nutritional Computing Concepts, Inc.
Taste-Testing—Robyn Webb Associates

Printed in the United States of America

The suggestions and information contained in this publication are generally consistent with the *Clinical Practice Recommendations* and other policies of the American Diabetes Association, but they do not represent the policy or position of the Association or any of its boards or committees. Reasonable steps have been taken to ensure the accuracy of the information presented. However, the American Diabetes Association cannot ensure the safety or efficacy of any product or service described in this publication. Individuals are advised to consult a physician or other appropriate health care professional before undertaking any diet or exercise program or taking any medication referred to in this publication. Professionals must use and apply their own professional judgment, experience, and training and should not rely solely on the information contained in this publication before prescribing any diet, exercise, or medication. The American Diabetes Association—its officers, directors, employees, volunteers, and members—assumes no responsibility or liability for personal or other injury, loss, or damage that may result from the suggestions or information in this publication.

American Diabetes Association
1660 Duke Street
Alexandria, Virginia 22314

Library of Congress Cataloging-in-Publication Data

The complete quick & hearty diabetic cookbook / American Diabetes Association.
        p.   cm.
    Includes index.
    ISBN 1-58040-002-7 (pbk.)
    1. Diabetes--Diet therapy--Recipes.   I. American Diabetes Association.   II. Title:
Complete quick and hearty diabetic cookbook.
    RC662.C63   1998
    641.5'6314--DC21   97-46530
                                                                                    CIP

John T. Devlin, MD
Maine Medical Center
Portland, Maine

Alan M. Jacobson, MD
Joslin Diabetes Center
Boston, Massachusetts

Lois Jovanovic, MD
Sansum Medical Research Foundation
Santa Barbara, California

Carolyn Leontos, MS, RD, CDE
The University of Nevada Cooperative Extension
Las Vegas, Nevada

Peter A. Lodewick, MD
Diabetes Care Center
Birmingham, Alabama

Carol E. Malcom, BSN, CDE
Highline Community Hospital
Seattle, Washington

Wylie McNabb, EdD
The University of Chicago Center for Medical
    Education and Health Care
Chicago, Illinois

Virginia Peragallo-Dittko, RN, MA, CDE
Winthrop University Hospital
Mineola, New York

Jacqueline Siegel, RN
St. Joseph Hospital
Seattle, Washington

Tim Wysocki, PhD
Nemours Children's Clinic
Jacksonville, Florida

CONTENTS

FOREWORD

Packed with tasty and easy-to-prepare recipes, *The Complete Quick & Hearty Diabetic Cookbook* is a terrific addition to your cookbook library. Here are some important points to keep in mind as you try the recipes:

+ The nutrient analysis section *only includes* the ingredients listed in the ingredients section! The nutrient analyses do *not* include serving suggestions sometimes provided in other sections of the recipe. For example, in the recipe for Broiled Shrimp with Garlic, we suggest that it be served over rice. But, because rice is not included as an ingredient, you know that the nutrient analysis only applies to the Broiled Shrimp recipe itself. Similarly, suggested garnishes are not included in the analyses (unless they are included in the ingredients list).

+ In general, we have suggested using olive oil instead of low-calorie margarine. You can use low-calorie margarine if you prefer, depending on your individual nutrition goals. Olive oil provides more monounsaturated fats, but low-calorie margarine contains fewer calories. Feel free to interchange them if you need to.

+ If you can find a version of an ingredient lower in fat than the items we used, feel free to use it instead. The recipes will still work, and your total fat grams will go down slightly. We usually use low-fat options, defined as containing 3 grams of fat or less per serving. When we use the term low-calorie, that means 40 calories or less per serving.

+ Remember that when a food is listed as a Free Food, there may still be limits on the serving size. For example, for many dressings and toppings, only 2 Tbsp or less is free. More than that, and the food has an exchange value. Also, in terms of nutrient values, 1 Starch Exchange can be interchanged with 1 Fruit Exchange.

+ Be aware that the heat stability of sugar substitutes can vary, depending on the brand of sweetener used. You need to make sure the sugar substitute of your choice can be baked or heated without changing flavor. Product manufacturers can tell you this. Also, note that the serving sizes are not uniform and vary from recipe to recipe.

Good luck, and we hope you enjoy *The Complete Quick & Hearty Diabetic Cookbook!*

APPETIZERS

BAKED SCALLOPS

4 servings/serving size: 3 oz

Spear these scallops with fancy toothpicks or serve them on a bed of butter lettuce as a prelude to a pasta dish. Remember not to overcook scallops; they become chewy instead of tender.

- ◆ **12 oz fresh bay or sea scallops**
- ◆ **1/2 tsp salt (optional)**
- ◆ **1-1/2 tsp pickling spices**
- ◆ **1/2 cup cider vinegar**
- ◆ **1/4 cup water**
- ◆ **1 Tbsp finely chopped onion**
- ◆ **1 head butter lettuce**

1. Preheat the oven to 350 degrees. Wash the scallops in cool water and cut any scallops that are too big in half.
2. Spread scallops out in a large baking dish (be careful not to overlap them). Combine the spices, cider vinegar, water, and onion together in a small bowl and pour the mixture over the scallops.
3. Cover the baking dish and bake for 7 minutes. Remove from the oven and allow the scallops to cool in the refrigerator (leave them in the cooking liquid).
4. Just before serving, place lettuce leaves on individual plates or a platter and serve.

....

Lean Meat Exchange 1	Total Carbohydrate . . . . 2 grams	
Calories 70	Dietary Fiber . . . . 1 gram	
Total Fat . . . . 1 gram	Sugars . . . . 1 gram	
Saturated Fat . . . . 0 grams	Protein . . . . 13 grams	
Calories from Fat 8	Sodium . . . . 216 milligrams	
Cholesterol . . . . 29 milligrams	w/o added salt . . . . . 152 milligrams	

BROILED SHRIMP
WITH GARLIC

12 servings/serving size: 2-1/2 oz

You can prepare this fast appetizer as guests are walking in, or serve it as a main course over rice. Make sure you buy 2 pounds of unshelled shrimp!

- 2 lb large shrimp, unshelled
- 1/3 cup olive oil
- 1 Tbsp lemon juice
- 1/4 cup chopped scallions
- 1 Tbsp chopped garlic
- 2 tsp fresh ground pepper
- 1 large lemon, sliced
- 4 Tbsp chopped fresh parsley

1. Set the oven to broil. Shell uncooked shrimp, but do not remove the tails. With a small knife, split the shrimp down the back and remove the vein. Wash the shrimp with cool water and pat dry with paper towels.
2. In a medium skillet, over medium heat, heat the olive oil. Add the lemon juice, scallions, garlic, and fresh pepper. Heat the mixture for 3 minutes. Set aside.
3. Arrange the shrimp in a baking dish and pour the olive oil mixture over the shrimp. Broil the shrimp 4 to 5 inches from the heat for 2 minutes per side just until the shrimp turns bright pink. Transfer the shrimp to a platter and garnish with lemon slices and parsley. Pour the juices from the pan over the shrimp.

....

Lean Meat Exchange 2	Total Carbohydrate . . . . 1 gram
Calories 115	Dietary Fiber . . . . 0 grams
Total Fat . . . . 7 grams	Sugars . . . . 0 grams
Saturated Fat . . . . 1 gram	Protein . . . . 13 grams
Calories from Fat 60	Sodium . . . . 139 milligrams
Cholesterol . . . . 120 milligrams	

CHEESY TORTILLA WEDGES

12 servings/serving size: 1/2 of a corn tortilla (3 wedges)
with 1 Tbsp guacamole

These wedges are like nachos, except they are much lower in fat and calories!

- **6 large corn tortillas**
- **1 Tbsp olive oil**
- **1 cup shredded low-fat cheddar cheese**
- **1 cup shredded low-fat Monterey Jack cheese**

- **1/2 cup green chiles**
- **1/2 cup sliced pitted black olives**
- **Guacamole** (see recipe, page 14)

1. Preheat the oven to 400 degrees. Spread both sides of tortilla with olive oil. Place on cookie sheets and bake 3 minutes or until lightly browned.
2. Turn tortillas over; top with the two cheeses, chiles, and olives, spreading to the edge. Bake an additional 3 minutes or until cheese melts.
3. Cut each tortilla into 6 wedges and arrange on a platter. Top with guacamole and serve.

Starch Exchange 1/2	Cholesterol . . . . 16 milligrams
Medium-Fat Meat Exchange 1	Total Carbohydrate . . . . 9 grams
Fat Exchange 1	Dietary Fiber . . . . 2 grams
Calories 144	Sugars . . . . 3 grams
Total Fat . . . . 10 grams	Protein . . . . 6 grams
Saturated Fat . . . . 4 grams	Sodium . . . . 232 milligrams
Calories from Fat 86	

CHERRY TOMATOES STUFFED WITH CRAB

12 servings/serving size: 3 cherry tomatoes

These bite-sized morsels with a fresh crabmeat filling are easy to make and easy to eat.

- ◆ **36 large cherry tomatoes**
- ◆ **1 tsp salt**
- ◆ **1/4 cup low-fat cottage cheese**
- ◆ **1-1/2 tsp minced onion**
- ◆ **1/2 tsp prepared horseradish**
- ◆ **1-1/2 tsp fresh lemon juice**
- ◆ **1/8 tsp garlic powder**

- ◆ **1/2 lb (8 oz) fresh crabmeat, drained and flaked**
- ◆ **1/4 cup minced celery**
- ◆ **1 Tbsp finely chopped green pepper**
- ◆ **Parsley leaves**

1. Cut the tops off the tomatoes with a small knife and remove the pulp with a small spoon (use demitasse spoons, if you have them, or a small spoon with a pointed tip).
2. Sprinkle the insides of each tomato with salt. Invert the tomatoes on paper towels and let them drain while you prepare the filling.
3. Place the cottage cheese in a food processor or blender and process until smooth (about 2 minutes). Add the onion, horseradish, lemon juice, and garlic powder and process 1 more minute. Stir in the crabmeat, celery, and green pepper.
4. Stuff each tomato with some of the crabmeat filling. Arrange on a serving platter and refrigerate for at least 1 hour before serving. Garnish each tomato with a parsley leaf.

....

Vegetable Exchange 1	Total Carbohydrate . . . . 3 grams
Calories 35	Dietary Fiber . . . . 1 gram
Total Fat . . . . 0 grams	Sugars . . . . 2 gram
Saturated Fat . . . . 0 grams	Protein . . . . 5 grams
Calories from Fat 4	Sodium . . . . 275 milligrams
Cholesterol . . . . 8 milligrams	

CHICKEN KABOBS

6 servings/serving size: 2 skewers (2 to 2-1/2 oz)

If you use wooden skewers for your kabobs, be sure to soak them in hot water 15 minutes before threading the chicken. This prevents the skewers from burning under the broiler or on the barbeque.

- ◆ **1 lb boneless, skinless chicken breast**
- ◆ **3 Tbsp lite soy sauce**
- ◆ **1 1-inch cube of fresh ginger root, finely chopped**
- ◆ **3 Tbsp olive oil**
- ◆ **3 Tbsp dry vermouth**
- ◆ **1 large clove garlic, finely chopped**
- ◆ **12 watercress sprigs**
- ◆ **2 large lemons, cut into wedges**

1. Cut chicken into 1-inch cubes and place in a shallow bowl. Combine all the marinade ingredients and pour over the chicken. Cover the chicken and let marinate overnight.
2. Thread the chicken onto 12 skewers. Grill or broil 6 inches from the heat source for 8 minutes, turning frequently. Arrange skewers on a platter and garnish with watercress and lemon wedges. Serve hot with additional soy sauce, if desired.

....

Lean Meat Exchange 2	Total Carbohydrate . . . . 0 grams
Calories 105	Dietary Fiber . . . . 0 grams
Total Fat . . . . 4 grams	Sugars . . . . 0 grams
Saturated Fat . . . . 1 gram	Protein . . . . 17 grams
Calories from Fat 32	Sodium . . . . 115 milligrams
Cholesterol . . . . 46 milligrams	

CHILLED SHRIMP

20 servings/serving size: 2-1/2 oz

Your guests will appreciate this nicely chilled shrimp in a pretty combination of red onion, parsley, and lemon. Make sure you buy 5 pounds of unshelled shrimp!

- 5 lb jumbo shrimp, unshelled
- 1/4 cup plus 2 Tbsp olive oil
- 4 medium lemons, thinly sliced
- 3 Tbsp minced garlic
- 3 medium red onions, thinly sliced
- 1/2 cup minced parsley
- Parsley sprigs

1. Peel and devein shrimp, leaving tails intact.
2. Preheat the oven to 400 degrees. Arrange the shrimp on a baking sheet and brush with 2 Tbsp olive oil. Bake the shrimp for 3 minutes or until they turn bright pink.
3. Place the lemon slices in a large bowl. Add the remaining 1/4 cup of olive oil, garlic, onions, and minced parsley. Add the shrimp and toss vigorously to coat. Cover and let marinate, refrigerated, for 6 to 8 hours.
4. Just before serving, arrange the shrimp on a serving platter. Garnish with parsley sprigs and some of the red onions and lemons from the bowl.

....

Lean Meat Exchange 2
Calories 94
Total Fat . . . . 3 grams
  Saturated Fat . . . . 0 grams
  Calories from Fat 26
Cholesterol . . . . 151 milligrams

Total Carbohydrate . . . . 0 grams
  Dietary Fiber . . . . 0 grams
  Sugars . . . . 0 grams
Protein . . . . 16 grams
Sodium . . . . 174 milligrams

CRAB CAKES

6 servings/serving size: 2-1/2 oz (2 cakes)

Golden brown and full of flavor, crab cakes are great the night of your party, and you can use the leftovers to make crab cake sandwiches the next day!

- 1 lb (16 oz) fresh crabmeat, shelled and cartilage removed
- 2 Tbsp finely minced parsley
- 2 Tbsp skim milk
- 1/2 tsp cayenne pepper
- 1/2 tsp dry mustard
- 2 Tbsp finely chopped onion
- 2 Tbsp finely chopped celery
- 2 egg substitute equivalents
- 1/2 tsp freshly ground pepper
- 8 slices low-calorie bread, crusts removed and finely crumbled
- 10 unsalted crackers, crushed into crumbs

1. In a medium bowl, combine all the ingredients except the cracker crumbs. Coat a baking sheet with nonstick cooking spray; set aside.
2. Shape the crabmeat mixture into 12 patties about 3 inches in diameter and 1/2 inch thick. Coat each patty with the cracker crumbs and place on the baking dish. Refrigerate the crab cakes 1 hour before baking. Preheat the oven to 400 degrees.
3. Bake the crab cakes at 400 degrees for 8 minutes or until golden brown. Transfer to a serving platter and serve hot.

....

Starch Exchange	1	Cholesterol	65 milligrams
Lean Meat Exchange	1	Total Carbohydrate	15 grams
Calories	151	Dietary Fiber	3 grams
Total Fat	2 grams	Sugars	2 grams
Saturated Fat	0 grams	Protein	18 grams
Calories from Fat	22	Sodium	361 milligrams

CRAB-FILLED MUSHROOMS

10 servings/serving size: 2 mushrooms

This is a very versatile filling you can also stuff into cherry tomatoes or zucchini or yellow squash "boats" (cut 2-inch pieces of squash and scoop out the middle).

- **20 large fresh mushroom caps, cleaned** (to clean mushrooms, dust off any dirt on the cap with a mushroom brush or paper towels), **stems removed**
- **6 oz canned or fresh crabmeat, rinsed, drained, and flaked**
- **2 Tbsp chopped fresh parsley**
- **2 Tbsp dried bread crumbs** (see recipe, page 217)
- **2 Tbsp finely chopped green onion**
- **Fresh ground pepper**
- **1/4 cup chopped pimentos**
- **3 Tbsp olive oil**

1. In a small mixing bowl, combine the crabmeat, parsley, bread crumbs, green onion, and pepper.
2. Place the cleaned and stemmed mushroom caps in a 13x9x2-inch baking dish crown side down. Stuff some of the crabmeat filling into each cap. Place a little pimento on top of the filling. Cover and refrigerate overnight.
3. Drizzle olive oil over each cap. Bake at 350 degrees for 15 to 17 minutes. Transfer to a serving platter and serve hot.

....

Vegetable Exchange 1	Cholesterol . . . . 15 milligrams
Fat Exchange 1	Total Carbohydrate . . . . 3 grams
Calories 66	Dietary Fiber . . . . 1 gram
Total Fat . . . . 5 grams	Sugars . . . . 1 gram
Saturated Fat . . . . 1 gram	Protein . . . . 4 grams
Calories from Fat 41	Sodium . . . . 53 milligrams

CREAMY TARRAGON DIP

5 servings/serving size: 2 Tbsp

This dip resembles a French boursin; it's especially good if you refrigerate it for 1 to 2 hours before serving to let the flavors blend.

- ◆ 2 tsp fresh or 1 tsp dried tarragon
- ◆ 2 tsp minced scallions
- ◆ 2 tsp minced parsley
- ◆ 1 cup low-fat cottage cheese
- ◆ 2 Tbsp tarragon vinegar
- ◆ 2 Tbsp low-fat cream cheese, softened
- ◆ 1 tsp Dijon mustard

Combine all the ingredients in a food processor and process until smooth. Refrigerate until guests arrive; serve with raw vegetables or crackers.

....

Lean Meat Exchange	1	Total Carbohydrate	3 grams
Calories	55	Dietary Fiber	0 grams
Total Fat	2 grams	Sugars	2 grams
Saturated Fat	1 gram	Protein	7 grams
Calories from Fat	17	Sodium	229 milligrams
Cholesterol	7 milligrams		

CUCUMBER PATÉ

12 servings/serving size: 1/2 cup

You might want to make this tasty paté the day before your party, so it can solidify in the refrigerator overnight.

- 1 large cucumber, peeled, seeded, and chopped
- 1 small green pepper, seeded and quartered
- 1 cup chopped celery
- 1 medium onion, quartered
- 1 cup low-fat cottage cheese
- 1/2 cup low-fat mayonnaise
- 1 pkg. unflavored gelatin
- 1/4 cup boiling water
- 1/4 cup cold water
- Assorted crackers

1. Spray a 5-cup mold or a 1-1/2–quart mixing bowl with nonstick cooking spray.
2. In a food processor, coarsely chop the cucumber, green pepper, celery, and onion. Remove the vegetables from the food processor and set aside. Combine the cottage cheese and mayonnaise in the food processor and blend until smooth.
3. In a medium bowl, dissolve the gelatin in boiling water; slowly stir in the cold water. Add the chopped vegetables and cottage cheese mixture and mix thoroughly.
4. Pour the mixture into the prepared mold and refrigerate overnight or until firm. To serve, carefully invert mold onto serving plate and remove the mold. Surround the paté with assorted crackers.

••

Vegetable Exchange	1	Cholesterol	6 milligrams
Fat Exchange	1	Total Carbohydrate	4 grams
Calories	61	Dietary Fiber	1 gram
Total Fat	4 grams	Sugars	3 grams
Saturated Fat	1 gram	Protein	4 grams
Calories from Fat	32	Sodium	146 milligrams

FRESH DILL DIP

6 servings/serving size: 2 Tbsp

The fresh dill really adds great flavor to this dip.

- 1 cup plain nonfat yogurt
- 1/2 tsp salt (optional)
- 1/4 tsp fresh ground pepper
- 1/4 cup minced parsley
- 2 Tbsp chopped fresh chives
- 1 Tbsp chopped fresh dill
- 1 Tbsp apple cider vinegar
- Fresh cut vegetables

In a small bowl, combine all the ingredients. Chill for 2 to 4 hours. Serve with fresh cut vegetables.

....

Free Food*
Calories 17
Total Fat .... 0 grams
  Saturated Fat .... 0 grams
  Calories from Fat 1
Cholesterol .... 1 milligram

Total Carbohydrate .... 2 grams
  Dietary Fiber .... 0 grams
  Sugars .... 2 grams
Protein .... 2 grams
Sodium .... 208 milligrams
  w/o added salt .... 3 milligrams

*Remember that only 2 Tbsp or less is a Free Food!

GRUYERE APPLE SPREAD

10 servings/serving size: 2 Tbsp

We've left the heavy ingredients out of this rich spread, tasty with crackers or fresh, raw vegetables.

- **4 oz (1/2 cup) Neufchatel cheese**
- **1/2 cup low-fat cottage cheese**
- **1/2 cup Gruyere cheese**
- **1/4 tsp dry mustard**
- **1/2 cup shredded apple (unpeeled)**

- **2 Tbsp finely chopped pecans**
- **2 tsp minced chives**
- **Assorted crackers or celery stalks**

1. Place the cheeses in a food processor and blend until smooth. Add the mustard and blend for 30 seconds.
2. Transfer the mixture to a serving bowl and fold in the apple and pecans. Sprinkle the dip with chives.
3. Cover and refrigerate the mixture for 1 to 2 hours. Serve chilled with crackers or stuff into celery stalks.

....

Medium-Fat Meat Exchange 1
Calories 74
Total Fat . . . . 6 grams
  Saturated Fat . . . . 3 grams
  Calories from Fat 50
Cholesterol . . . . 16 milligrams

Total Carbohydrate . . . . 2 grams
  Dietary Fiber . . . . 0 grams
  Sugars . . . . 1 gram
Protein . . . . 4 grams
Sodium . . . . 109 milligrams

GUACAMOLE

8 servings/serving size: 1/4 cup

There's a secret to selecting perfectly ripe avocados: look for slightly blackened ones that give just a little when you press on their skins.

- 2 large ripe avocados, peeled, pit removed, and mashed
- 1/2 chopped onion
- 2 medium jalapeno chile peppers, seeded and chopped
- 2 Tbsp minced fresh parsley
- 2 Tbsp fresh lime juice
- 1/8 tsp fresh ground pepper
- 2 medium tomatoes, finely chopped
- 1 medium garlic clove, minced
- 1 Tbsp olive oil
- 1/2 tsp salt (optional)

In a large mixing bowl, combine all ingredients, blending well. Cover and refrigerate for at least 1 to 2 hours.

....

Vegetable Exchange 1	Total Carbohydrate . . . . 9 grams
Fat Exchange 2-1/2	Dietary Fiber . . . . 5 grams
Calories 132	Sugars . . . . 3 grams
Total Fat . . . . 11 grams	Protein . . . . 2 grams
Saturated Fat . . . . 2 grams	Sodium . . . . 146 milligrams
Calories from Fat 102	w/o added salt . . . . . . 11 milligrams
Cholesterol . . . . 0 milligrams	

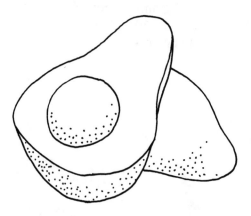

HOT ARTICHOKE DIP

32 servings/serving size: 2 Tbsp

Fresh Parmesan cheese gives this dip a special flavor.

- 2 15-oz cans artichoke hearts, packed in water, drained
- 2 cloves garlic
- 2 Tbsp olive oil
- 1/3 cup fresh lemon juice
- 1/4 tsp hot pepper sauce
- 1/4 cup grated fresh Parmesan cheese

- 2 cups finely ground bread crumbs
- 1/2 tsp dried oregano
- 1/2 tsp dried basil
- 1/4 tsp paprika
- 1/4 tsp dried thyme

1. Preheat the oven to 350 degrees. In a blender or food processor, puree the first five ingredients for 30 seconds. Pour the puree into a large bowl; stir in the cheese, bread crumbs, and herbs. Transfer the mixture to a 1-quart baking dish.
2. Cover the dip and bake for 15 minutes or until lightly golden brown. Serve warm with crackers or bread.

....

Starch Exchange	1/2	Total Carbohydrate	6 grams
Calories	41	Dietary Fiber	1 gram
Total Fat	1 gram	Sugars	1 gram
Saturated Fat	0 grams	Protein	2 grams
Calories from Fat	13	Sodium	128 milligrams
Cholesterol	1 milligram		

HOT CRAB DIP

6 servings/serving size: 1/3 cup

This dip is delicious with chunks of thick, crusty sourdough bread.

- **7 oz canned or fresh crabmeat, rinsed, drained, and flaked**
- **1/2 tsp horseradish**
- **1/4 tsp paprika**
- **8 oz (1 cup) low-fat cream cheese**
- **1 Tbsp skim milk**
- **2 Tbsp fresh lemon juice**
- **Assorted crackers**

1. Preheat the oven to 350 degrees. In a medium bowl, combine all ingredients, blending thoroughly.
2. Spoon mixture into a small casserole dish and bake for 15 minutes until mixture bubbles. Serve hot with crackers.

Lean Meat Exchange 1
Fat Exchange 1
Calories 111
Total Fat . . . . 7 grams
    Saturated Fat . . . . 4 grams
    Calories from Fat 65
Cholesterol . . . . 49 milligrams
Total Carbohydrate . . . . 3 grams
    Dietary Fiber . . . . 0 grams
    Sugars . . . . 3 grams
Protein . . . . 10 grams
Sodium . . . . 295 milligrams

HUMMUS

12 servings/serving size: 2 Tbsp

*T*his recipe for this traditional Middle Eastern dip contains a lot less fat than other recipes; it's delicious with raw carrots or pita bread.

- ◆ 1 15-oz can chickpeas, drained (reserve a little liquid)
- ◆ 3–6 garlic cloves
- ◆ Juice of 1 lemon
- ◆ Juice of 1 lime
- ◆ 1 tsp olive oil
- ◆ 1 tsp ground cumin

Combine all ingredients in a blender or food processor until smooth, adding chickpea liquid if necessary to blend. Refrigerate. Serve with crunchy vegetables, crackers, or pita bread.

....

Starch Exchange	1/2	Total Carbohydrate	8 grams
Calories	49	Dietary Fiber	1 gram
Total Fat	1 gram	Sugars	2 grams
Saturated Fat	0 grams	Protein	2 grams
Calories from Fat	9	Sodium	39 milligrams
Cholesterol	0 milligrams		

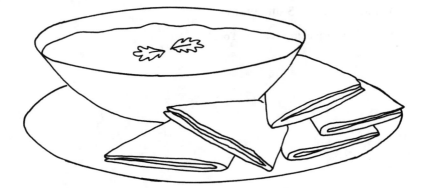

LOW-FAT CREAM CHEESE DIP

80 servings/serving size: 1 Tbsp

You can use this basic recipe in several different ways. As written, it's perfect when you need plain cream cheese to serve with bagels. Add minced herbs such as parsley or chives (or pureed berries) to make flavored cream cheese. The frosting recipe with fructose added (see page 256) is delicious on baked goods!

- 1-1/3 cups plain nonfat yogurt, strained overnight in cheese-cloth over a bowl set in the refrigerator
- 3 cups skim milk ricotta cheese
- 2 cups low-fat cottage cheese

Combine all the ingredients in a food processor; process until smooth. Place in a covered container and refrigerate until ready to use (this cream cheese can be refrigerated for up to 1 week).

. . . .

Free Food*
Calories 20
Total Fat . . . . 1 gram
   Saturated Fat . . . . 1 gram
   Calories from Fat 8
Cholesterol . . . . 3 milligrams

Total Carbohydrate . . . . 1 gram
   Dietary Fiber . . . . 0 grams
   Sugars . . . . 1 gram
Protein . . . . 2 grams
Sodium . . . . 37 milligrams

*Remember that only 1 Tbsp or less is a Free Food!

MONTEREY JACK CHEESE QUICHE SQUARES

12 servings/serving size: one 3-inch square

The green chiles add a special flavor to this delicious quiche.

- ◆ 3 egg substitute equivalents
- ◆ 1 cup plus 2 Tbsp cottage cheese
- ◆ 1/4 cup plus 2 Tbsp flour
- ◆ 3/4 tsp baking powder

- ◆ 1 cup shredded Monterey Jack cheese
- ◆ 1/2 cup diced green chiles
- ◆ 2 Tbsp diced red pepper
- ◆ Parsley sprigs

1. Preheat the oven to 350 degrees. Beat egg substitutes and cottage cheese together in a medium bowl for 2 minutes until smooth.
2. Add the flour and baking powder and beat until smooth. Stir in the cheese, green chiles, and red pepper.
3. Coat a square 9-inch pan with nonstick cooking spray and pour in egg mixture. Bake for 30 to 35 minutes until firm.
4. Remove the quiche from the oven and allow to cool for 10 minutes (it will be easier to cut). Cut into squares and transfer to a platter, garnish with parsley sprigs, and serve.

....

Starch Exchange 1/2	Cholesterol . . . . 176 milligrams
Lean Meat Exchange 1	Total Carbohydrate . . . . 4 grams
Calories 75	Dietary Fiber . . . . 0 grams
Total Fat . . . . 3 grams	Sugars . . . . 1 gram
Saturated Fat . . . . 2 grams	Protein . . . . 7 grams
Calories from Fat 30	Sodium . . . . 176 milligrams

STUFFED SHRIMP

8 servings/serving size: 1 shrimp

This recipe calls for butterflied shrimp. Your fish market will do this for you if you wish—or simply make a deeper knife cut and flatten the jumbo shrimp after peeling and deveining.

- 1 cup seasoned bread crumbs
- 2 Tbsp dry vermouth
- 1 Tbsp grated fresh Parmesan cheese
- 1-1/2 tsp minced fresh parsley
- 1/4 cup olive oil
- 1 Tbsp paprika
- 1 garlic clove, minced
- 8 jumbo shrimp, shelled, deveined, and butterflied
- 1 medium lemon, sliced into wedges

1. Preheat the oven to 400 degrees. Coat a large baking dish with nonstick cooking spray or lightly grease with olive oil or margarine.
2. In a small bowl, combine the bread crumbs, vermouth, Parmesan cheese, parsley, olive oil, paprika, and garlic. Mix thoroughly.
3. In the baking dish, arrange the shrimp, cut side up. Mound the filling equally among all the shrimp, pressing to compact filling.
4. Bake the shrimp for 7 to 8 minutes or until the tops are golden brown.
5. Transfer the shrimp to a platter and garnish with lemon wedges.

....

Starch Exchange	1	Cholesterol	90 milligrams
Lean Meat Exchange	1	Total Carbohydrate	11 grams
Fat Exchange	1/2	Dietary Fiber	1 gram
Calories	164	Sugars	1 gram
Total Fat	8 grams	Protein	12 grams
Saturated Fat	1 gram	Sodium	512 milligrams
Calories from Fat	70		

TURKEY MEATBALLS

20 servings/serving size: 2–3 meatballs

Serve this with some marinara sauce—it's a healthy version of a great Italian appetizer.

- **1 lb ground turkey**
- **1/4 cup low-sodium chicken broth**
- **1/4 tsp allspice**
- **1 slice low-calorie bread, finely crumbled**
- **1 egg substitute equivalent**
- **4 tsp fresh lemon juice**
- **1/4 tsp ground nutmeg**
- **2 Tbsp finely chopped green onion**
- **1/2 tsp grated lemon peel**
- **1-1/4 cups marinara sauce** (find the low-sodium, low-fat, sugarless version in the supermarket)

1. Preheat the oven to 400 degrees. Coat a shallow baking dish with nonstick cooking spray and set aside.
2. Combine all the ingredients except the marinara sauce in a medium bowl, mixing thoroughly. Form the mixture into tiny meatballs, about 1 tsp each.
3. Place the meatballs on the baking sheet and bake for 10 minutes or until well browned all over. Remove from the oven and arrange on a serving platter. Spear each turkey meatball with a fancy toothpick. Serve with 1 Tbsp of marinara sauce per serving.

....

Lean Meat Exchange 1	Total Carbohydrate . . . . 2 grams
Calories 47	Dietary Fiber . . . . 0 grams
Total Fat . . . . 2 grams	Sugars . . . . 1 gram
Saturated Fat . . . . 1 gram	Protein . . . . 5 grams
Calories from Fat 21	Sodium . . . . 27 milligrams
Cholesterol . . . . 12 milligrams	

DRESSINGS &
SAUCES

BASIC BARBECUE SAUCE

12 servings/serving size: 2 Tbsp

Use this version instead of bottled, and you will agree homemade has its benefits. Store in the freezer.

- 1 Tbsp olive oil
- 1 medium onion, chopped
- 1-1/4 cups tomato sauce
- 1 bay leaf
- 1/4 tsp curry powder

- Fresh ground pepper
- 1 Tbsp white vinegar
- 1/4 tsp dry mustard
- 1/4 tsp hot pepper sauce
- 1 Tbsp chopped parsley

1. In a medium saucepan, heat the oil and saute the onion until tender, about 5 minutes. Add the remaining ingredients and simmer for 20 minutes.
2. Discard the bay leaf and transfer the sauce to a container.

....

Vegetable Exchange 1	Total Carbohydrate . . . . 3 grams
Calories 24	Dietary Fiber . . . . 0 grams
Total Fat . . . . 1 gram	Sugars . . . . 2 grams
Saturated Fat . . . . 0 grams	Protein . . . . 1 gram
Calories from Fat 11	Sodium . . . . 6 milligrams
Cholesterol . . . . 0 milligrams	

BASIC VINAIGRETTE

24 servings/serving size: 1 Tbsp

*S*pice up this basic dressing with chopped, fresh herbs such as basil or dill.

- ◆ 3/4 cup olive oil
- ◆ 3 Tbsp fresh lemon juice
- ◆ 1 garlic clove, minced
- ◆ 2 Tbsp white wine vinegar

- ◆ 2 tsp Dijon mustard
- ◆ 1 tsp minced fresh parsley
- ◆ Dash salt and pepper

Combine all ingredients in a blender or food processor. Process until well blended. Refrigerate until ready to use.

Fat Exchange 1-1/2	Total Carbohydrate . . . . 0 grams
Calories 61	Dietary Fiber . . . . 0 grams
Total Fat . . . . 7 grams	Sugars . . . . 0 grams
Saturated Fat . . . . 1 gram	Protein . . . . 0 grams
Calories from Fat 61	Sodium . . . . 11 milligrams
Cholesterol . . . . 0 milligrams	

CREAMY HERB DRESSING

24 servings/serving size: 1 Tbsp

Use this low-fat, low-calorie creamy dressing over salad greens or as a dip for vegetables.

- 1/2 cup plain nonfat yogurt
- 1 cup low-fat cottage cheese
- 1-1/2 tsp fresh lemon juice
- 1 medium carrot, peeled and grated
- 2 tsp grated onion
- 1/2 tsp thyme
- 1/4 tsp marjoram
- 1/4 tsp oregano
- 1/4 tsp basil
- 1/4 tsp salt (optional)

In a food processor, combine the yogurt, cottage cheese, and lemon juice; process until smooth. Pour into a small mixing bowl. Add the remaining ingredients and mix well. Cover and refrigerate for 1 to 2 hours before serving.

....

Free Food*
Calories 11
Total Fat . . . . 0 grams
   Saturated Fat . . . . 0 grams
   Calories from Fat 2
Cholesterol . . . . 43 milligrams

Total Carbohydrate . . . . 1 gram
   Dietary Fiber . . . . 0 grams
   Sugars . . . . 1 gram
Protein . . . . 2 grams
Sodium . . . . 64 milligrams
   w/o added salt . . . . . . 43 milligrams

*Remember that only 2 Tbsp or less is a Free Food!

DILL DRESSING

16 servings/serving size: 1 Tbsp

Try this dressing with fresh grilled salmon or swordfish.

- 1/2 cup plain nonfat yogurt
- 2 Tbsp low-fat mayonnaise
- 2 tsp grated onion
- 1 garlic clove, minced
- 1/4 cup skim milk

- 1 tsp dried dill or 2 tsp chopped fresh dill
- 1/4 tsp dried oregano
- Fresh ground pepper

Combine all ingredients in a food processor or blender and process until smooth. Pour into a container, cover, and refrigerate for 1 to 2 hours before serving.

··

Free Food*
Calories . . . . ⁻10
Total Fat . . . . 1 gram
 Saturated Fat . . . . 0 grams
 Calories from Fat 5
Cholesterol . . . . 1 milligram

Total Carbohydrate . . . . 1 gram
 Dietary Fiber . . . . 0 grams
 Sugars . . . . 1 gram
Protein . . . . 0 grams
Sodium . . . . 18 milligrams

*Remember that only 2 Tbsp or less is a Free Food!

FRENCH DRESSING

12 servings/serving size: 1 Tbsp

This dressing makes a special impression on dinner guests, with its pleasing aroma and pretty color.

- **1/2 cup olive oil**
- **1/4 cup malt vinegar**
- **1 tsp salt (optional)**
- **Dash lemon pepper**
- **Dash paprika**
- **1/4 tsp dry mustard**

Combine all ingredients in a blender or food processor. Process until well blended. Refrigerate until ready to use.

....

Fat Exchange	2	Total Carbohydrate	0 grams
Calories	80	Dietary Fiber	0 grams
Total Fat	9 grams	Sugars	0 grams
Saturated Fat	1 gram	Protein	0 grams
Calories from Fat	81	Sodium	178 milligrams
Cholesterol	0 milligrams	w/o added salt	0 milligrams

GINGER SOY DRESSING

16 servings/serving size: 1 Tbsp

*T*his dressing can double as a marinade for chicken, turkey, or fish.

- 1/2 cup lite soy sauce
- 2 Tbsp sesame oil
- 2 Tbsp rice vinegar
- 1 Tbsp grated fresh ginger

- 1 Tbsp dry sherry
- 1 tsp granulated sugar
  substitute

Combine all ingredients in a small jar, cover tightly, and shake vigorously until well blended. Keep covered and refrigerated until ready to serve. Shake again before serving.

....

Fat Exchange 1/2
Calories 20
Total Fat . . . . 2 grams
   Saturated Fat . . . . 0 grams
   Calories from Fat 15
Cholesterol . . . . 0 milligrams

Total Carbohydrate . . . . 1 gram
   Dietary Fiber . . . . 0 grams
   Sugars . . . . 1 gram
Protein . . . . 0 grams
Sodium . . . . 300 milligrams

MARINARA SAUCE

20 servings/serving size: 1/4 cup

Keep a batch on hand in the freezer. The taste compliments shrimp or pasta and is a great dipping sauce for baked chicken fingers.

- ◆ **24 oz tomato puree**
- ◆ **1 green pepper, chopped**
- ◆ **1/2 cup minced onion**
- ◆ **1 tsp dried oregano**
- ◆ **1/2 lb mushrooms, sliced**
- ◆ **1 red pepper, chopped**
- ◆ **1 tsp dried basil**
- ◆ **1/2 tsp garlic powder**

In a large saucepan over medium heat, combine all ingredients, mixing thoroughly. Let simmer 40 to 50 minutes, allowing flavors to blend.

....

Vegetable Exchange 1	Total Carbohydrate . . . . 5 grams
Calories 19	Dietary Fiber . . . . 0 grams
Total Fat . . . . 0 grams	Sugars . . . . 2 grams
Saturated Fat . . . . 0 grams	Protein . . . . 1 gram
Calories from Fat 0	Sodium . . . . 135 milligrams
Cholesterol . . . . 0 milligrams	

MOCK HOLLANDAISE

4 servings/serving size: 2 Tbsp

Use over any fresh, lightly steamed vegetable.

- 1/2 cup low-calorie low-fat mayonnaise
- 3 Tbsp water

- 1 Tbsp lemon juice
- Fresh ground white pepper

1. In a small saucepan, combine all ingredients. Whisk until smooth.
2. Simmer mixture over low heat, stirring constantly, for 3 to 4 minutes until heated through.

....

Fat Exchange	2	Total Carbohydrate	2 grams
Calories	101	Dietary Fiber	0 grams
Total Fat	9 grams	Sugars	1 gram
Saturated Fat	1 gram	Protein	0 grams
Calories from Fat	83	Sodium	221 milligrams
Cholesterol	12 milligrams		

PARMESAN DRESSING

16 servings/serving size: 1 Tbsp

This dressing also tastes good with cooked broccoli, string beans, or asparagus.

- ◆ **1/2 cup white wine vinegar**
- ◆ **3 Tbsp grated Parmesan cheese**
- ◆ **1 garlic clove, minced**
- ◆ **Dash salt (optional)**
- ◆ **1/2 cup olive oil**
- ◆ **1 tsp dried basil**
- ◆ **Fresh ground pepper**

Place all ingredients in a jar and cover. Shake vigorously and refrigerate until ready to use.

....

Fat Exchange 1-1/2
Calories 65
Total Fat . . . . 7 grams
   Saturated Fat . . . . 1 gram
   Calories from Fat 63
Cholesterol . . . . 1 milligram

Total Carbohydrate . . . . 1 gram
   Dietary Fiber . . . . 0 grams
   Sugars . . . . 1 gram
Protein . . . . 0 grams
Sodium . . . . 26 milligrams
   w/o added salt . . . . . . 18 milligrams

TANGY MARINADE

Makes 1-2/3 cups/use 1/3 cup per recipe

*G*reat *for marinating beef or pork before grilling. Store extra portions in the freezer.*

- 1 cup unsweetened pineapple juice
- 1 garlic clove, minced
- 1/3 cup lite soy sauce
- 1 tsp ground ginger
- 1/3 cup low-calorie Italian salad dressing

In a shallow dish, combine all ingredients, mixing thoroughly. Keep refrigerated until ready to use.

....

Starch Exchange	1/2	Total Carbohydrate	9 grams
Calories	44	Dietary Fiber	0 grams
Total Fat	0 grams	Sugars	9 grams
Saturated Fat	0 grams	Protein	1 gram
Calories from Fat	0	Sodium	870 milligrams
Cholesterol	0 milligrams		

SALADS

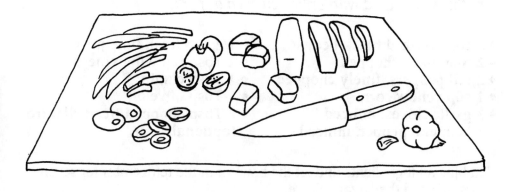

BLACK BEAN SALAD

8 servings/serving size: 1 cup

Try this spicy salad with grilled chicken or pork.

- 3 cups cooked black beans
- 2 tomatoes, chopped
- 2 red peppers, finely chopped
- 1 cup yellow corn
- 3 garlic cloves, minced
- 1 jalapeno pepper, minced
- 1/4 cup fresh lime juice
- 2 Tbsp red wine vinegar
- 1 Tbsp cumin
- 1 Tbsp olive oil
- 2 Tbsp chopped fresh cilantro (optional)

Combine all ingredients and let the bowl sit in the refrigerator for several hours to blend the flavors. Serve.

....

Starch Exchange 1-1/2	Cholesterol .... 0 milligrams
Vegetable Exchange 1	Total Carbohydrate .... 26 grams
Calories 145	Dietary Fiber .... 7 grams
Total Fat .... 2 grams	Sugars .... 7 grams
Saturated Fat .... 0 grams	Protein .... 7 grams
Calories from Fat 22	Sodium .... 77 milligrams

CALIFORNIA SEAFOOD SALAD

8 servings/serving size: 4 oz

*T*ry *using pieces of crab or lobster instead of, or in addition to, the shrimp and scallops.*

- 1/4 lb fresh green beans, cut into 1-inch pieces
- 1 Tbsp olive oil
- 1 lb fresh scallops
- 1 lb uncooked fresh shrimp, peeled and deveined
- 1/2 cup low-fat sour cream
- 2 Tbsp low-fat mayonnaise

- 2 Tbsp skim milk
- 1 Tbsp chopped fresh dill
- 2 Tbsp chopped fresh parsley
- 2 Tbsp fresh lime juice
- 1 head romaine lettuce
- 1 large tomato, cut into wedges
- 1 lemon, cut into wedges

1. To prepare the salad, steam the green beans for 3 to 4 minutes until cooked, but slightly crunchy. Set aside. In a large skillet, heat the olive oil.
2. Add the scallops and shrimp and saute over medium heat for 4 to 5 minutes until the seafood is cooked (the shrimp turn pink and the scallops are no longer translucent). Set aside to cool while you prepare the dressing.
3. Combine all the dressing ingredients together in a small bowl. Add the dressing to the seafood and mix well. Add the green beans and toss again.
4. To assemble, place lettuce leaves on individual plates or one platter. Place seafood salad in a mound on top of the lettuce. Surround the salad with tomato and lemon wedges.

....

Vegetable Exchange 1	Cholesterol . . . . 87 milligrams
Lean Meat Exchange 2	Total Carbohydrate . . . . 7 grams
Calories 143	Dietary Fiber . . . . 2 grams
Total Fat . . . . 5 grams	Sugars . . . . 4 grams
Saturated Fat . . . . 1 gram	Protein . . . . 18 grams
Calories from Fat 45	Sodium . . . . 226 milligrams

CHINESE CHICKEN SALAD

8 servings/serving size: 3–4 oz

This is a crunchy salad, loaded with sweet pineapple and crisp water chestnuts.

- **2 cups cooked chicken, diced**
- **1 cup finely chopped celery**
- **1/4 cup crushed unsweetened pineapple, drained**
- **2 Tbsp finely diced pimentos**
- **2 8-oz cans water chestnuts, drained and chopped**
- **2 scallions, chopped**
- **1/3 cup low-fat mayonnaise**
- **1 Tbsp lite soy sauce**
- **1 tsp lemon juice**
- **8 large tomatoes, hollowed**

1. In a large bowl, combine the chicken, pineapple, pimentos, celery, water chestnuts, and scallions.
2. In a separate bowl, combine the mayonnaise, soy sauce, and lemon juice. Mix well. Add the dressing to the salad and toss. Cover and refrigerate for 2 to 3 hours.
3. For each serving, place a small scoop of chicken salad into a hollowed-out tomato. You may also stuff the chicken salad into celery stalks or serve on bread.

....

Starch Exchange* 1	Cholesterol .... 35 milligrams
Lean Meat Exchange 1	Total Carbohydrate .... 14 grams
Fat Exchange 1/2	Dietary Fiber .... 3 grams
Calories 155	Sugars .... 10 grams
Total Fat .... 6 grams	Protein .... 12 grams
Saturated Fat .... 1 gram	Sodium .... 196 milligrams
Calories from Fat 57	

*Instead of 1 Starch Exchange, you can use 3 Vegetable Exchanges.

COUSCOUS SALAD

3 servings/serving size: 1 cup

Couscous, also known as Moroccan pasta, is very simple to prepare. Place dry couscous in a heat-proof bowl, pour double the amount of boiling water or broth over it, and let it sit for 5 to 10 minutes until all the water is absorbed.

- **1 cup couscous, rehydrated (see above)**
- **1/4 cup finely chopped red or yellow pepper**
- **1/4 cup chopped carrots**
- **1/4 cup finely chopped celery**
- **2 Tbsp minced Italian parsley**
- **1 Tbsp olive oil**
- **4 Tbsp rice vinegar**
- **2 garlic cloves, minced**
- **3 Tbsp finely minced scallions**
- **Fresh ground pepper**

Combine the couscous, vegetables, and minced parsley together in a large bowl. Combine the remaining ingredients in a blender or food processor and process for 1 minute. Pour over the couscous and vegetables, toss well, and serve.

....

Starch Exchange	2	
Fat Exchange	1/2	
Calories	191	
Total Fat	5 grams	
Saturated Fat	1 gram	
Calories from Fat	42	

Cholesterol	0 milligrams
Total Carbohydrate	32 grams
Dietary Fiber	2 grams
Sugars	4 grams
Protein	5 grams
Sodium	20 milligrams

CRAB AND RICE SALAD

4 servings/serving size: 1/4 recipe

*B*rown rice gives this salad a great nutty taste.

- ♦ **1 cup uncooked brown rice**
- ♦ **5 oz fresh steamed crabmeat, flaked**
- ♦ **1 large tomato, diced**
- ♦ **1/4 cup chopped green pepper**
- ♦ **3 Tbsp chopped fresh parsley**
- ♦ **2 Tbsp red onion**

- ♦ **1/2 cup plain nonfat yogurt**
- ♦ **1-1/2 Tbsp lemon juice**
- ♦ **1/4 tsp salt (optional)**
- ♦ **Fresh ground pepper**
- ♦ **1 head butter lettuce**
- ♦ **1 large tomato, cut into wedges**

1. In a medium saucepot, boil 2-1/2 cups of water. Slowly add 1 cup uncooked brown rice. Cover and reduce the heat to low. Cook the rice for 45 to 50 minutes until tender. Do not continually stir the rice (this will cause it to become gummy). Just check occasionally.
2. In a large salad bowl, combine all the ingredients except the lettuce and tomato wedges. Just before serving, line plates with the lettuce and spoon salad on top of the lettuce. Garnish with tomato wedges.

Starch Exchange	2	Total Carbohydrate	31 grams
Vegetable Exchange	1	Dietary Fiber	4 grams
Calories	190	Sugars	6 grams
Total Fat	2 grams	Protein	13 grams
Saturated Fat	0 grams	Sodium	273 milligrams
Calories from Fat	18	w/o added salt	139 milligrams
Cholesterol	37 milligrams		

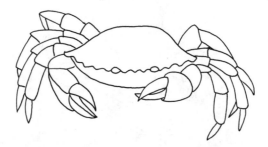

FRESH SEAFOOD PASTA SALAD

12 servings/serving size: 3/4 cup

This is a delicious medley of fresh fish, pasta, and vegetables.

- 3/4 cup broccoli florets
- 22 oz uncooked fresh shrimp, peeled and deveined
- 1 lb cooked small pasta shells
- 2 medium carrots, peeled and diced
- 1/2 medium red onion, diced
- 4 Tbsp chopped cilantro
- 1 each red, yellow, and green pepper, julienned
- 8 large cherry tomatoes, halved
- 4 medium celery stalks, diced
- 4 scallions, chopped
- 2 Tbsp minced garlic
- 12 large pitted black olives
- 1/2 lb cooked sea scallops
- 1/2 lb precooked crab legs
- 1/2 cup olive oil
- 1/3 cup red wine vinegar
- Fresh ground pepper

1. Blanch broccoli florets by placing in boiling water. Turn off the heat, wait 1 minute and drain the broccoli. Pour cool water over the broccoli to stop the cooking process and drain again.
2. Boil the shrimp until it just turns pink. Combine the pasta and vegetables in a large salad bowl. Add the cooked seafood and toss with the pasta and vegetables.
3. Combine the oil, vinegar, and pepper. Pour the dressing over the salad and refrigerate for several hours before serving.

....

Starch Exchange	1	
Vegetable Exchange	1	
Medium-Fat Meat Exchange	1	
Fat Exchange	1	
Calories	226	
Total Fat	11 grams	
Saturated Fat	2 grams	
Calories from Fat	97	

Cholesterol	90 milligrams
Total Carbohydrate	17 grams
Dietary Fiber	2 grams
Sugars	5 grams
Protein	16 grams
Sodium	242 milligrams

GREEK POTATO SALAD

10 servings/serving size: 1/2 cup

You'll love this unique potato salad, served warm, with its authentic flavor of Kalamata olives (Greek olives). Find them at your supermarket or a gourmet deli.

- 1/3 cup olive oil
- 4 garlic cloves, minced
- 2 lb red potatoes, cut into 1-1/2–inch pieces (leave the skin on if you wish)
- 6 medium carrots, peeled, halved lengthwise, and cut into 1-1/2–inch pieces
- 1 onion, chopped
- 16 oz artichoke hearts packed in water, drained and cut in half
- 1/2 cup Kalamata olives, pitted and halved
- 1/4 cup lemon juice
- Dash salt and pepper

1. In a large skillet, heat the olive oil, add the garlic, and saute for 30 seconds. Add the potatoes, carrots, and onion; cook over medium heat for 25 to 30 minutes until vegetables are tender.
2. Add the artichoke hearts and cook for 3 to 5 minutes more. Remove from heat and stir in the olives and lemon juice. Season with salt and pepper. Transfer to a serving bowl and serve warm.

....

Starch Exchange 1	Cholesterol .... 0 milligrams
Vegetable Exchange 1	Total Carbohydrate .... 25 grams
Fat Exchange 1-1/2	Dietary Fiber .... 4 grams
Calories 177	Sugars .... 4 grams
Total Fat .... 8 grams	Protein .... 3 grams
Saturated Fat .... 1 gram	Sodium .... 237 milligrams
Calories from Fat 74	

GREEN BEAN, WALNUT, AND FETA SALAD*

6 servings/serving size: 1/2 cup

*M*ake sure to toast the walnuts—the roasted flavor really enhances this salad.

- 1/2 cup walnuts
- 1-1/2 lb fresh green beans, trimmed and halved
- 1 medium red onion, sliced into rings
- 1/2 cup peeled, seeded, and diced cucumber
- 1/3 cup crumbled feta cheese
- 1/4 cup olive oil
- 1/4 cup white wine vinegar
- 1/4 cup chopped fresh mint leaves
- 1 garlic clove, minced
- 1/2 tsp salt (optional)

1. Toast the walnuts by placing them in a small baking dish in a 300-degree oven for 10 minutes until lightly browned. Remove from the oven and set aside.
2. Cook the green beans by placing them in a pot of boiling water and then turning off the heat. Do not allow the green beans to boil in the water. Immediately drain and run cool water over the beans to stop the cooking process. This method will help retain their green color and crunchy texture.
3. In a salad bowl, combine the green beans with the walnuts, red onion rings, cucumber and feta cheese. Combine all the dressing ingredients together and toss with the vegetables. Chill 2 to 3 hours before serving.

....

Vegetable Exchange	2	Total Carbohydrate	13 grams
Fat Exchange	3-1/2	Dietary Fiber	4 grams
Calories	217	Sugars	4 grams
Total Fat	18 grams	Protein	5 grams
Saturated Fat	4 grams	Sodium	320 milligrams
Calories from Fat	158	w/o added salt	142 milligrams
Cholesterol	11 milligrams		

*This salad is high in fat.

ITALIAN POTATO SALAD

6 servings/serving size: 1/2 cup

The warm, earthy taste of balsamic vinegar gives this salad its punch. Leave the skins on the red potatoes for a rustic look.

- ◆ 24 new red potatoes, 3–4 oz each, washed and skins left on
- ◆ 3 celery stalks, chopped
- ◆ 1 red pepper, minced
- ◆ 1/4 cup chopped scallions
- ◆ 2 Tbsp olive oil
- ◆ 1 Tbsp balsamic vinegar
- ◆ 1/2 Tbsp red vinegar
- ◆ 1 tsp chopped fresh parsley
- ◆ Fresh ground pepper

1. Boil the potatoes for 20 minutes in a large pot of boiling water. Drain and let cool for 30 minutes. Cut potatoes into large chunks and toss the potatoes with the celery, red pepper, and scallions.
2. Combine all the dressing ingredients and pour over the potato salad. Serve at room temperature.

....

Starch Exchange 1
Vegetable Exchange 1
Fat Exchange 1/2
Calories 122
Total Fat . . . . 5 grams
  Saturated Fat . . . . 1 gram
  Calories from Fat 42

Cholesterol . . . . 0 milligrams
Total Carbohydrate . . . . 19 grams
  Dietary Fiber . . . . 3 grams
  Sugars . . . . 1 gram
Protein . . . . 2 grams
Sodium . . . . 29 milligrams

LENTIL SALAD

8 servings/serving size: 1 cup

*T*he flavor of this filling salad improves with time, so you can leave the leftovers in the refrigerator for 2 to 3 days and serve it again!

- 1 lb dried lentils, washed (rinse with cold water in a colander)
- 3 cups water
- 2 Tbsp olive oil
- 2 tsp cumin
- 1 tsp minced fresh oregano
- 3 Tbsp fresh lemon juice

- Fresh ground pepper
- 2 large green peppers, cored, seeded, and diced
- 2 large red peppers, cored, seeded, and diced
- 3 stalks celery, diced
- 1 red onion, minced

1. In a large saucepan over high heat, bring lentils and water to a boil. Reduce the heat to low, cover, and simmer for 35 to 45 minutes. Drain and set aside.
2. In a large bowl, mix together the oil, lemon juice, cumin, oregano, and pepper until well blended. Add the lentils and the prepared vegetables. Cover and refrigerate before serving.

Starch Exchange 2-1/2	Cholesterol . . . . 0 milligrams
Vegetable Exchange 1	Total Carbohydrate . . . . 38 grams
Fat Exchange 1/2	Dietary Fiber . . . . 14 grams
Calories 238	Sugars . . . . 8 grams
Total Fat . . . . 4 grams	Protein . . . . 15 grams
Saturated Fat . . . . 1 gram	Sodium . . . . 26 milligrams
Calories from Fat 40	

LOBSTER SALAD

6 servings/serving size: 1/2 cup

Lobster is a special treat your guests will appreciate!

- 2 lb lobster in the shell or
  1 lb lobster meat
- 3/4 lb small red potatoes
- 1/2 cup low-fat mayonnaise
- 3 Tbsp plain low-fat yogurt

- 1 Tbsp chopped tarragon
- 1/4 cup chopped scallions
- Fresh ground pepper
- 1 small head romaine lettuce,
  washed and leaves separated

1. To prepare lobster in the shell, place the lobster in boiling water and boil until meat is tender, about 20 minutes. Cool the lobster, remove the meat from the shell, and cut into 1-inch cubes. You may also purchase lobster meat from the seafood department at the supermarket.
2. Wash, but do not peel the potatoes. Boil the potatoes in water until tender, about 15–20 minutes. Drain, cool, and quarter. In a bowl, combine the remaining dressing ingredients. In a separate bowl, combine the lobster and potatoes.
3. Add dressing to the lobster and potatoes and mix well. To serve, line plates with lettuce. Spoon lobster salad over the lettuce.

....

Starch Exchange 1	Cholesterol . . . . 63 milligrams
Lean Meat Exchange 2	Total Carbohydrate . . . . 15 grams
Calories 193	Dietary Fiber . . . . 2 grams
Total Fat . . . . 7 grams	Sugars . . . . 2 grams
Saturated Fat . . . . 1 gram	Protein . . . . 18 grams
Calories from Fat 61	Sodium . . . . 417 milligrams

MEDITERRANEAN CHICKEN SALAD

3 servings/serving size: 3 oz

*T*ry adding very thin slices of feta cheese to this salad to give it more of a Greek flair!

- ◆ **8 oz boneless, skinless, cooked chicken breast**
- ◆ **3 Tbsp olive oil**
- ◆ **2 Tbsp balsamic vinegar**
- ◆ **1/4 tsp dried basil**
- ◆ **2 small garlic cloves, minced**
- ◆ **Fresh ground pepper**
- ◆ **1 cup cooked green beans, cut into 2-inch lengths**
- ◆ **1/4 cup sliced black olives**
- ◆ **4 cherry tomatoes, halved**

1. Cut the cooked chicken into bite-sized chunks and set aside. In a medium bowl, whisk together the oil, vinegar, basil, garlic, and pepper. Add the chicken and toss with dressing.
2. Add the green beans, olives, and cherry tomatoes; toss well. Refrigerate for several hours. Garnish salad with tomato wedges and serve.

••

Medium-Fat Meat Exchange 3	Cholesterol .... 67 milligrams
Vegetable Exchange 1	Total Carbohydrate .... 7 grams
Fat Exchange 1	Dietary Fiber .... 2 grams
Calories 304	Sugars .... 3 grams
Total Fat .... 21 grams	Protein .... 23 grams
Saturated Fat .... 4 grams	Sodium .... 247 milligrams
Calories from Fat 186	

OVERNIGHT COLESLAW

6 servings/serving size: about 1 cup

This salad gets all its flavor from spices and apple juice instead of high-fat mayonnaise.

- ◆ 4 cups shredded cabbage (green or purple or a mixture)
- ◆ 2 cups shredded carrots
- ◆ 3/4 cup sliced scallions
- ◆ 3/4 cup unsweetened apple juice
- ◆ 2/3 cup cider vinegar

- ◆ 1-1/2 tsp paprika
- ◆ 1 tsp mustard seeds
- ◆ 1/2 tsp garlic powder
- ◆ 1/2 tsp celery seeds
- ◆ Fresh ground pepper
- ◆ 1 Tbsp dry mustard

1. Combine the cabbage, carrots, and scallions.
2. Combine the remaining ingredients in a blender and pour over the cabbage mixture. Toss to coat. Refrigerate overnight and serve chilled.

....

Vegetable Exchange	2	Total Carbohydrate	12 grams
Calories	47	Dietary Fiber	2 grams
Total Fat	0 grams	Sugars	9 grams
Saturated Fat	0 grams	Protein	1 gram
Calories from Fat	0	Sodium	22 milligrams
Cholesterol	0 milligrams		

PASTA SALAD-STUFFED TOMATOES

4 servings/serving size: 2/3 cup stuffing in 1 medium tomato

This is a lovely salad to serve for a light luncheon.

- 1 cup uncooked corkscrew macaroni
- 2 small carrots, sliced
- 2 scallions, chopped
- 2 oz pimentos, drained
- 1 cup cooked kidney beans
- 1/2 cup sliced celery
- 1/4 cup cooked peas
- 2 Tbsp chopped fresh parsley
- 1/4 cup low-calorie Italian salad dressing
- 2 Tbsp low-fat mayonnaise
- 1/4 tsp dried marjoram
- Fresh ground pepper
- 4 medium tomatoes

1. Cook the corkscrew macaroni in boiling water until cooked, about 7 to 8 minutes; drain. In a large mixing bowl, combine the macaroni with the remaining salad ingredients and toss well. Cover and chill 1 hour or more.
2. With the stem end down, cut each tomato into 6 wedges, cutting to, but not through, the base of the tomato. Spread wedges slightly apart; spoon pasta mixture into tomatoes. Chill until ready to serve.

....

Starch Exchange	2	Cholesterol	3 milligrams
Vegetable Exchange	1	Total Carbohydrate	37 grams
Fat Exchange	1/2	Dietary Fiber	7 grams
Calories	207	Sugars	9 grams
Total Fat	4 grams	Protein	8 grams
Saturated Fat	1 gram	Sodium	303 milligrams
Calories from Fat	34		

SHANGHAI SALAD

4 servings/serving size: 1 cup

*U*se last night's leftover steak to create this warm Asian salad.

- 3 Tbsp canola oil
- 1 tsp grated ginger
- 1 garlic clove, minced
- 8 oz cooked lean flank steak, cut into 1-inch pieces
- 1-1/2 cups fresh snow peas, trimmed
- 1 8-oz can water chestnuts, drained and sliced
- 6 scallions, cut into 2-inch pieces
- 2 Tbsp dry sherry
- 1 Tbsp lite soy sauce
- 1 head romaine lettuce, shredded

1. In a large skillet, heat the oil over medium-high heat. Saute the ginger and garlic for 1 to 2 minutes.
2. Add the remaining ingredients to the skillet and stir until heated through.
3. Arrange shredded lettuce on platter, spoon mixture over the bed of lettuce, and serve.

Vegetable Exchange 2
Medium-Fat Meat Exchange 2
Fat Exchange 1-1/2
Calories 267
Total Fat . . . . 16 grams
   Saturated Fat . . . . 3 grams
   Calories from Fat 148

Cholesterol . . . . 38 milligrams
Total Carbohydrate . . . . 10 grams
   Dietary Fiber . . . . 3 grams
   Sugars . . . . 7 grams
Protein . . . . 18 grams
Sodium . . . . 204 milligrams

SHRIMP AND RADICCHIO SALAD

4 servings/serving size: about 1/3 cup

Radicchio is a very beautiful lettuce—its burgundy color adds eye appeal to any salad!

- ◆ 1/4 cup olive oil
- ◆ 2 Tbsp red wine vinegar
- ◆ 3 medium garlic cloves, minced
- ◆ 1 medium shallot, minced
- ◆ 2 tsp Dijon mustard
- ◆ 1 tsp prepared horseradish

- ◆ Fresh ground pepper
- ◆ 1/2 lb cooked bay shrimp
- ◆ 1 medium head Boston lettuce, shredded
- ◆ 1 medium head radicchio lettuce, shredded

1. In a medium bowl, combine all the dressing ingredients. Add the shrimp and toss well. Refrigerate for 30 minutes.
2. Just before serving, combine the lettuce and radicchio in a serving bowl. Place the shrimp mixture on top, toss, and serve.

....

Vegetable Exchange	1	Cholesterol	111 milligrams
Lean Meat Exchange	2	Total Carbohydrate	5 grams
Fat Exchange	1-1/2	Dietary Fiber	2 grams
Calories	202	Sugars	2 grams
Total Fat	14 grams	Protein	14 grams
Saturated Fat	2 grams	Sodium	186 milligrams
Calories from Fat	130		

TABBOULEH SALAD

8 servings/serving size: 1/2 cup

*Y*ou can find the bulgur wheat called for in this recipe in most supermarkets (look in the rice and pasta aisle).

- 1 cup bulgur wheat
- 2 cups boiling water
- 1 large tomato, chopped
- 1/2 cup minced fresh parsley
- 1/4 cup chopped scallions
- 1 Tbsp chopped fresh mint

- 1/4 cup fresh lemon juice
- Dash salt and pepper
- 1 Tbsp olive oil
- 1 tsp ground cumin
- 1 small head butter lettuce
- 1 lemon, cut into wedges

1. In a small bowl, combine the wheat with the boiling water and let stand at room temperature for at least 1 hour, until the wheat has absorbed the water. The wheat will expand and should yield about 2 cups of rehydrated wheat.
2. Combine the tomato, parsley, scallions, and mint with the wheat and toss well. Combine the dressing ingredients and pour over the wheat salad. Cover and refrigerate overnight or for at least 2–3 hours.
3. To serve, place lettuce leaves on individual plates and spoon salad over lettuce leaves. Garnish with lemon wedges.

....

Starch Exchange 1	Cholesterol . . . . 0 milligrams
Vegetable Exchange 1	Total Carbohydrate . . . . 20 grams
Calories 104	Dietary Fiber . . . . 1 gram
Total Fat . . . . 2 grams	Sugars . . . . 7 grams
Saturated Fat . . . . 0 grams	Protein . . . . 3 grams
Calories from Fat 19	Sodium . . . . 29 milligrams

TORTELLINI AND FETA CHEESE SALAD*

6 servings/serving size: 1/2 cup

A *little bit of this salad goes a long way—it's packed with tortellini, walnuts, and feta cheese!*

- 1/4 cup olive oil
- 1/4 cup white wine vinegar
- 1/4 cup sliced scallions
- 3 garlic cloves, minced
- 1 Tbsp dried basil
- 1 tsp dried dill
- 24 oz frozen tortellini, stuffed with cheese

- 8-oz can water-packed artichoke hearts, drained and quartered
- 1/3 cup crumbled feta cheese
- 1/4 cup chopped black olives
- 1/4 cup chopped walnuts
- 1 large tomato, quartered

1. In a small bowl, whisk together the oil and vinegar. Add scallions, cloves, basil, and dill; mix well.
2. Combine the remaining ingredients and pour the dressing on top. Refrigerate overnight or at least 2 to 3 hours. Serve.

Starch Exchange 3
Lean Meat Exchange 1
Fat Exchange 3
Calories 420
Total Fat . . . . 22 grams
  Saturated Fat . . . . 6 grams
  Calories from Fat 198

Cholesterol . . . . 51 milligrams
Total Carbohydrate . . . . 45 grams
  Dietary Fiber . . . . 3 grams
  Sugars . . . . 5 grams
Protein . . . . 14 grams
Sodium . . . . 537 milligrams

*This recipe is high in fat.

WILD RICE SALAD

4 servings/serving size: 1 cup

This salad has a slightly sweet flavor.

- 1 cup raw wild rice (rinsed)
- 4 cups cold water
- 1 cup mandarin oranges, packed in their own juice (drain and reserve 2 Tbsp of liquid)
- 1/2 cup chopped celery
- 1/4 cup minced red pepper
- 1 shallot, minced
- 1 tsp minced thyme
- 2 Tbsp raspberry vinegar
- 1 Tbsp olive oil

1. Place the rinsed, raw rice and the water in a saucepan. Bring to a boil, lower the heat, cover the pan, and cook for 45 to 50 minutes until the rice has absorbed the water. Set the rice aside to cool.

2. In a large bowl, combine the mandarin oranges, celery, red pepper, and shallot. In a small bowl, combine the reserved juice, thyme, vinegar, and oil. Add rice to the mandarin oranges and vegetables. Pour the dressing over the salad, toss, and serve.

....

Starch Exchange 2-1/2
Calories 205
Total Fat . . . . 4 grams
   Saturated Fat . . . . 1 gram
   Calories from Fat 36
Cholesterol . . . . 0 milligrams

Total Carbohydrate . . . . 38 grams
   Dietary Fiber . . . . 5 grams
   Sugars . . . . 7 grams
Protein . . . . 6 grams
Sodium . . . . 22 milligrams

ZUCCHINI AND CARROT SALAD*

4 servings/serving size: about 1/2 cup

Julienned ribbons of carrot, zucchini, and fennel in a delightful Dijon vinaigrette.

- ◆ 2 medium carrots, peeled and julienned
- ◆ 1 medium zucchini, julienned
- ◆ 1/2 medium fennel bulb, core removed and julienned
- ◆ 1 Tbsp fresh orange juice
- ◆ 2 Tbsp Dijon mustard
- ◆ 3 Tbsp olive oil
- ◆ 1 tsp white wine vinegar
- ◆ 1/2 tsp dried thyme
- ◆ 1 Tbsp finely minced parsley
- ◆ Dash salt
- ◆ Fresh ground pepper
- ◆ 1/4 cup chopped walnuts
- ◆ 1 medium head romaine lettuce, washed and leaves separated

1. Place julienned vegetables in a medium bowl and set aside.
2. Combine remaining ingredients, except walnuts and lettuce, and mix well. Pour dressing over vegetables and toss. Add walnuts and mix again. Refrigerate until ready to serve.
3. To serve, line a bowl or plates with lettuce leaves, and spoon salad on top.

....

Vegetable Exchange	2	Cholesterol	0 milligrams
Fat Exchange	3	Total Carbohydrate	10 grams
Calories	181	Dietary Fiber	5 grams
Total Fat	15 grams	Sugars	4 grams
Saturated Fat	2 grams	Protein	3 grams
Calories from Fat	137	Sodium	155 milligrams

*This recipe is high in fat.

SOUPS &
STEWS

CHICKEN AND MUSHROOM SOUP

6 servings/serving size: 1 cup

*T*ry *serving this soup with fresh Buttermilk Biscuits (see recipe, page 213).*

- ◆ 1 quart low-sodium chicken broth
- ◆ 1 Tbsp lite soy sauce
- ◆ 1 cup sliced mushrooms, stems removed
- ◆ 1 Tbsp finely chopped scallions
- ◆ 1 Tbsp dry sherry
- ◆ 1/2 lb boneless, skinless chicken breast, cubed

1. Simmer all ingredients except the chicken in a stockpot for 10 minutes.
2. Add the chicken cubes and simmer for 6 to 8 minutes more. Serve with additional soy sauce if desired (but be aware that this will raise the sodium level of the soup!).

....

Vegetable Exchange 1	Cholesterol . . . . 24 milligrams
Lean Meat Exchange 1	Total Carbohydrate . . . . 2 grams
Calories 74	Dietary Fiber . . . . 0 grams
Total Fat . . . . 2 grams	Sugars . . . . 1 gram
Saturated Fat . . . . 1 gram	Protein . . . . 10 grams
Calories from Fat 19	Sodium . . . . 159 milligrams

CHICKEN STEW WITH NOODLES

8 servings/serving size: 1 cup stew and 1/2 cup cooked noodles

*T*ry using this stew to top rice or a baked potato, too.

- 1 Tbsp olive oil
- 1 onion, chopped
- 2 garlic cloves, minced
- 1 lb boneless, skinless chicken breast, cubed
- 2 Tbsp flour
- 3 cups low-sodium chicken broth

- 1 cup dry white wine
- 1 Tbsp chopped fresh thyme (or 1 tsp dried)
- 1/2 cup minced parsley
- 1 lb cooked noodles, hot

add carrots, gr. beans celery

1. In a large saucepan, saute the onion and garlic in the oil for about 5 minutes. Add the chicken cubes and saute until chicken is cooked (about 10 minutes).
2. Sprinkle the flour over the chicken. Add the chicken broth, wine, and thyme. Bring to a boil, then lower the heat, and simmer for 30 minutes.
3. Toss together the noodles and the parsley. Pour the stew over the noodles and serve.

....

Starch Exchange	1	Cholesterol	53 milligrams
Lean Meat Exchange	2	Total Carbohydrate	19 grams
Calories	191	Dietary Fiber	1 gram
Total Fat	5 grams	Sugars	3 grams
Saturated Fat	1 gram	Protein	17 grams
Calories from Fat	42	Sodium	58 milligrams

CREAM OF CARROT SOUP

4 servings/serving size: 1 cup

This smooth, tasty soup is great to serve for special luncheons.

- 2 Tbsp low-sodium chicken broth
- 3 Tbsp finely chopped shallots or onions
- 2 Tbsp flour
- 1 cup skim milk, scalded and hot

- 1 tsp cinnamon
- 1 cup cooked, pureed carrots
- 1 cup low-sodium chicken broth
- Fresh ground pepper

1. Heat the broth in a stockpot over medium heat. Add shallots and cook until they are limp. Sprinkle shallots with flour and cook 2–3 minutes.
2. Pour in the hot milk and cook until mixture thickens. Add remaining ingredients. Bring almost to a boil, stirring often. Add pepper to taste.

....

Starch Exchange	1	Total Carbohydrate	13 grams
Calories	74	Dietary Fiber	2 grams
Total Fat	1 gram	Sugars	6 grams
Saturated Fat	0 grams	Protein	4 grams
Calories from Fat	6	Sodium	86 milligrams
Cholesterol	1 milligram		

ENGLISH BEEF STEW

8 servings/serving size: 1 cup

This stew has a slightly different flavor than Old-Fashioned Vegetable Beef Stew (see recipe, page 70), but is just as satisfying.

- ◆ 2 lb lean beef for stew, cut into large chunks
- ◆ 1-1/2 Tbsp flour
- ◆ 2 Tbsp canola oil
- ◆ 2 cups boiling water
- ◆ 2 tsp garlic powder
- ◆ 1 Tbsp Worcestershire sauce
- ◆ Dash salt and pepper
- ◆ 1 large yellow onion, quartered
- ◆ 4 large carrots, peeled and quartered
- ◆ 3 medium potatoes, white or russet, cut into 1-inch cubes
- ◆ 1 cup canned stewed tomatoes

1. Roll the beef cubes in the flour. In a large saucepan over medium heat, heat the canola oil. Add the beef and saute a few pieces of beef at a time. When all beef has been browned, add the boiling water to the pan.
2. Add the garlic powder, Worcestershire sauce, salt, and pepper. Lower the heat, cover, and let simmer for 2 to 2-1/2 hours or until the meat is very tender.
3. Add the onion, carrots, potatoes, and tomatoes. Let simmer about 30 minutes until all vegetables are tender. Transfer to a serving bowl and serve.

....

Starch Exchange	1	Cholesterol	65 milligrams
Lean Meat Exchange	3	Total Carbohydrate	20 grams
Calories	256	Dietary Fiber	3 grams
Total Fat	9 grams	Sugars	7 grams
Saturated Fat	2 grams	Protein	23 grams
Calories from Fat	82	Sodium	183 milligrams

FRENCH ONION SOUP

4 servings/serving size: 1 cup

*T*his version of a very popular soup is altered slightly—the fat content is much lower, yet the authentic taste is all here!

- ◆ **1 lb yellow onions, thinly sliced**
- ◆ **2 Tbsp olive oil**
- ◆ **1 tsp brown sugar substitute**
- ◆ **Fresh ground pepper**
- ◆ **Dash salt**
- ◆ **1 Tbsp unbleached flour**

- ◆ **1 qt low-sodium beef broth**
- ◆ **1/3 cup vermouth**
- ◆ **4 slices French bread, toasted (about 3/4-inch slices)**
- ◆ **1 cup shredded reduced-fat Swiss cheese**

1. In a large saucepot, saute the onion in the oil for 15 minutes. Add the sugar, pepper, and salt. Simmer uncovered for 35 minutes, stirring occasionally, adding a little water if necessary. The onions will get very brown.
2. Add the flour and cook an additional 1 minute. Gradually add the beef broth and vermouth; cook over medium heat, stirring constantly until thickened and bubbly. Reduce the heat and simmer for 20 minutes.
3. Ladle the soup into 4 individual oven-safe soup bowls. Top each bowl with a slice of bread and some cheese. Place under the broiler for 2 to 3 minutes. Carefully remove from the oven and serve.

....

Starch Exchange	2	Cholesterol	22 milligrams
Lean Meat Exchange	1	Total Carbohydrate	27 grams
Fat Exchange	2	Dietary Fiber	2 grams
Calories	307	Sugars	10 grams
Total Fat	15 grams	Protein	14 grams
Saturated Fat	6 grams	Sodium	261 milligrams
Calories from Fat	139		

FRESH FISH CHOWDER

6 servings/serving size: 1 cup

You can use almost any fish in this chowder—we've suggested halibut.

- 2 Tbsp olive oil
- 1 large garlic clove, minced
- 1 small onion, chopped
- 1 large green pepper, chopped
- 1 lb crushed tomatoes
- 1 Tbsp tomato paste
- 1/2 tsp dried basil
- 1/2 tsp dried oregano
- 1/4 cup dry red wine
- Dash salt and pepper
- 1/2 cup uncooked white rice
- 1/2 lb fresh halibut, cubed
- 2 Tbsp chopped parsley

1. Heat the olive oil in a 3-quart saucepan. Add the garlic, onion, and green pepper; saute for 10 minutes over low heat until vegetables are tender.
2. Add the tomatoes, tomato paste, basil, oregano, wine, salt, and pepper. Let simmer for 15 minutes. Add the rice and continue to cook for 15 minutes.
3. Add the halibut and cook for about 5 to 7 minutes until fish is cooked through. Garnish stew with chopped parsley and serve.

....

Starch Exchange	. . . .	1
Vegetable Exchange	. . . .	1
Medium-Fat Meat Exchange	. . . . . .	1
Calories	. . . .	181
Total Fat	. . . .	6 grams
Saturated Fat	. . . .	1 gram
Calories from Fat	. . . .	52

Cholesterol	. . . .	12 milligrams
Total Carbohydrate	. . . .	22 grams
Dietary Fiber	. . . .	2 grams
Sugars	. . . .	5 grams
Protein	. . . .	10 grams
Sodium	. . . .	72 milligrams

GAZPACHO

4 servings/serving size: 1-1/2 cups

Serve this cool, refreshing vegetable and tomato broth on hot summer days.

- 1 garlic clove, crushed
- 1 Tbsp olive oil
- 1 large onion, chopped
- 5 medium tomatoes, peeled
- 1 cup low-sodium chicken broth
- 2 Tbsp red wine vinegar
- 1 tsp hot pepper sauce
- 1/4 tsp paprika
- 1 large green or red pepper, chopped
- 1 cup peeled, seeded, and chopped cucumber
- 1/4 cup chopped scallions

1. Combine the garlic, oil, onion, and tomatoes in a food processor and process until smooth. Add the broth, vinegar, hot pepper sauce, and paprika; process again. Transfer the mixture to a large soup tureen or bowl.
2. Add the red or green pepper, cucumber, and scallions. Chill in the refrigerator overnight. Serve the soup in bowls or large wine glasses. Top with croutons if desired.

....

Starch Exchange 1	Cholesterol . . . . 1 milligram
Vegetable Exchange 1	Total Carbohydrate . . . . 20 grams
Fat Exchange 1/2	Dietary Fiber . . . . 5 grams
Calories 136	Sugars . . . . 14 grams
Total Fat . . . . 5 grams	Protein . . . . 6 grams
Saturated Fat . . . . 1 gram	Sodium . . . . 412 milligrams
Calories from Fat 44	

HEARTY VEGETABLE SOUP

8 servings/serving size: about 1 cup

*T*ry this soup with fresh-baked corn muffins (see recipe, page 214).

- 1-1/2 qt low-sodium chicken broth
- 28-oz can whole tomatoes, chopped and drained
- 1 cup chopped onion
- 1 cup diced potatoes
- 1 cup sliced carrots
- 1 cup yellow corn
- 1 cup frozen or fresh shelled peas

- 1 cup cooked kidney, black, or pinto beans (drained and rinsed, if canned)
- 2 tsp oregano
- 1 Tbsp minced fresh parsley
- 1 bay leaf
- Fresh ground pepper

Combine all ingredients in a large saucepot. Bring to a boil. Reduce the heat and simmer for 1 hour until vegetables are tender. Remove bay leaf before serving.

....

Starch Exchange 1-1/2
Vegetable Exchange 1
Calories 142
Total Fat . . . . 2 grams
   Saturated Fat . . . . 0 grams
   Calories from Fat 17
Cholesterol . . . . 1 milligram
Total Carbohydrate . . . . 26 grams
   Dietary Fiber . . . . 6 grams
   Sugars . . . . 7 grams
Protein . . . . 7 grams
Sodium . . . . 314 milligrams

ITALIAN MINESTRONE

8 servings/serving size: 1 cup

*T*his soup is traditionally served with warm, crusty French bread.

- 1 Tbsp olive oil
- 1/2 cup sliced onion
- 4 cups low-sodium chicken broth
- 3/4 cup sliced carrot
- 1/2 cup sliced potato (with peel)
- 2 cups sliced cabbage or coarsely chopped spinach
- 1 cup sliced zucchini
- 1/2 cup cooked garbanzo beans (drained and rinsed, if canned)
- 1/2 cup cooked navy beans (drained and rinsed, if canned)
- 16 oz canned tomatoes, with liquid
- 1/2 cup sliced celery
- 2 tsp dried basil
- 1 tsp dried oregano
- 1/2 cup uncooked rotini or other shaped pasta
- 1 Tbsp minced fresh parsley

1. In a large soup pot over medium heat, saute the onion in oil until onion is slightly browned. Add the chicken broth, carrot, and potatoes. Cover and cook over medium heat for 30 minutes.
2. Add remaining ingredients and cook for an additional 15 to 20 minutes until the pasta is cooked through.

Starch Exchange	1	Cholesterol	0 milligrams
Vegetable Exchange	1	Total Carbohydrate	19 grams
Calories	116	Dietary Fiber	4 grams
Total Fat	3 grams	Sugars	5 grams
Saturated Fat	0 grams	Protein	5 grams
Calories from Fat	25	Sodium	188 milligrams

LENTIL SOUP

8 servings/serving size: 1 cup

Cooking with lentils is a tasty and inexpensive way to include high-quality protein and complex carbohydrates in your diet—and they're easy to use because they don't require presoaking! This is a thick, hearty soup.

- ◆ 1 large onion, diced
- ◆ 1 large carrot, peeled and diced
- ◆ 2 stalks celery, diced
- ◆ 2 Tbsp olive oil
- ◆ 1 lb lentils
- ◆ 1-1/2 qt low-sodium chicken or beef broth
- ◆ 2 medium russet or white potatoes, peeled and diced
- ◆ 1 tsp oregano
- ◆ 1 tsp thyme
- ◆ Fresh ground pepper

1. In a stockpot or Dutch oven, saute the onion, carrot, and celery in the olive oil for 10 minutes. Add the lentils, broth, and potatoes.
2. Continue to cook for 30 to 45 minutes, adding the oregano and thyme 15 minutes before serving. Soup will keep for 3 days in the refrigerator or can be frozen for 3 months.

....

Starch Exchange 3
Fat Exchange 1/2
Calories 275
Total Fat .... 5 grams
  Saturated Fat .... 1 gram
  Calories from Fat 48

Cholesterol .... 1 milligram
Total Carbohydrate .... 42 grams
  Dietary Fiber .... 13 grams
  Sugars .... 7 grams
Protein .... 16 grams
Sodium .... 75 milligrams

MEXICAN TORTILLA SOUP

8 servings/serving size: 1 cup

*S*trips *of tortillas lace this spicy, hearty soup.*

- 2 tsp olive oil
- 1 onion, chopped
- 2 cloves garlic, minced
- 1 Tbsp chopped fresh cilantro
- 1 Tbsp cumin
- 1 tsp cayenne pepper
- 1 qt low-sodium chicken broth
- 1 15-oz can whole tomatoes, drained and coarsely chopped

- 1 medium zucchini, sliced
- 1 medium yellow squash, sliced
- 1 cup yellow corn
- 6 corn tortillas
- 8 Tbsp shredded low-fat cheese (optional)

1. In a large saucepan, saute the onion and garlic in the oil for 5 minutes.
2. Add the cilantro, cumin, and cayenne pepper; saute for 3 more minutes. Add remaining ingredients except the tortillas and optional cheese. Bring to a boil; cover and let simmer for 30 minutes.
3. Cut each tortilla into about 10 strips. Place the strips on a cookie sheet and bake for 5–6 minutes at 350 degrees until slightly browned and toasted. Remove from the oven.
4. To serve the soup, place strips of tortilla into each bowl. Ladle the soup on top of the tortilla strips. Top with cheese if desired.

....

Starch Exchange 1
Vegetable Exchange 1
(Fat Exchange) . . . . (1/2)*
Calories 113 (133)
Total Fat . . . . 3 (4) grams
  Saturated Fat . . . . 1 (1) gram
  Calories from Fat 24 (36)

Cholesterol . . . . 1 (6) milligram
Total Carbohydrate . . . 20 (21) grams
  Dietary Fiber . . . . 4 (4) grams
  Sugars . . . . 5 (5) grams
Protein . . . . 4 (6) grams
Sodium . . . . 190 (243) milligrams

*Values in parentheses indicate use of optional cheese.

MUSHROOM AND BARLEY SOUP

6 servings/serving size: 1 cup

Barley adds fiber and a rich flavor to soup.

- ◆ **1/2 cup barley**
- ◆ **6 cups water**
- ◆ **1 large carrot, diced**
- ◆ **2 cups diced celery**
- ◆ **2 bay leaves**
- ◆ **1/4 cup minced fresh parsley**
- ◆ **1 tsp dried thyme**

- ◆ **1 medium onion, diced**
- ◆ **2 Tbsp olive oil**
- ◆ **1/2 lb mushrooms, sliced**
- ◆ **1 garlic clove, minced**
- ◆ **2 Tbsp lite soy sauce**
- ◆ **2 Tbsp fresh lemon juice**
- ◆ **Fresh ground pepper**

1. Place barley and water in a 2-qt saucepan; bring to a boil. Reduce heat and let simmer; add carrot, celery, bay leaves, parsley, and thyme.

2. Return to a boil, reduce the heat, cover, and let simmer for 1 hour. When the barley has been cooking about 45 minutes, use a small skillet to saute the onion in the olive oil for about 5 minutes.

3. Add the mushrooms and saute until tender. Add the mushroom mixture to the barley, along with the remaining ingredients. Continue to simmer for 10 more minutes.

....

Starch Exchange 1-1/2	Cholesterol .... 0 milligrams
Fat Exchange 1/2	Total Carbohydrate .... 22 grams
Calories 140	Dietary Fiber .... 5 grams
Total Fat .... 5 grams	Sugars .... 5 grams
Saturated Fat .... 1 gram	Protein .... 3 grams
Calories from Fat 45	Sodium .... 262 milligrams

OLD-FASHIONED VEGETABLE BEEF STEW

8 servings/serving size: 1 cup

Loaded with chunky vegetables, this stew will warm you up on a cold day!

- 1 lb lean beef for stew, cut into 1-inch cubes
- 2 Tbsp olive oil
- 1 medium onion, diced
- 2 garlic cloves, crushed
- 28 oz canned tomatoes, slightly crushed
- 2 cups low-sodium beef broth
- 2 large carrots, peeled and cut into 1/4-inch round slices
- 1/2 lb mushrooms, sliced
- 1/2 lb green beans, cut into 2-inch pieces
- 4 celery stalks, sliced diagonally
- Fresh black pepper
- Dash cayenne pepper
- Dash hot pepper sauce
- 2 medium russet or white potatoes, peeled and cut into 1-inch cubes

1. In a large saucepan over medium heat, lightly brown the meat in the olive oil. Add the onion, garlic, tomatoes, and beef broth; bring to a boil.
2. Reduce to a simmer; add carrots, mushrooms, green beans, and celery. Season the soup with pepper, cayenne pepper, and hot pepper sauce. Cover and simmer for 45 minutes to 1 hour.
3. Add the potatoes and cook until tender, adding water if necessary. Serve hot.

....

Starch Exchange 1	Cholesterol . . . . 33 milligrams
Vegetable Exchange 1	Total Carbohydrate . . . . 20 grams
Lean Meat Exchange 1	Dietary Fiber . . . . 4 grams
Fat Exchange 1/2	Sugars . . . . 7 grams
Calories 193	Protein . . . . 14 grams
Total Fat . . . . 7 grams	Sodium . . . . 250 milligrams
Saturated Fat . . . . 2 grams	
Calories from Fat 64	

PASTA FAGIOLI

12 servings/serving size: 3/4–1 cup

*T*his hearty Italian soup freezes well, so you'll get several meals out of this recipe.

- 1 Tbsp olive oil
- 1 large onion, chopped
- 3 cloves garlic, crushed
- 2 medium carrots, sliced
- 2 medium zucchini, sliced
- 2 tsp basil
- 2 tsp oregano

- 32-oz can unsalted tomatoes with liquid
- 32-oz can white cannellini or navy beans, drained and rinsed
- 1 lb uncooked rigatoni or shell macaroni

1. Heat the oil in a large saucepan and saute the onions and garlic for 5 minutes.
2. Add the carrots, zucchini, basil, oregano, tomatoes with their liquid, and the beans. Cook until the vegetables are tender, about 15 to 17 minutes.
3. Cook the pasta according to package directions (without adding salt). Add the pasta and mix thoroughly. Serve warm with crusty bread.

....

Starch Exchange 3
Vegetable Exchange 1
Calories 263
Total Fat . . . . 2 grams
   Saturated Fat . . . . 0 grams
   Calories from Fat 19
Cholesterol . . . . 0 milligrams
Total Carbohydrate . . . . 51 grams
   Dietary Fiber . . . . 4 grams
   Sugars . . . . 10 grams
Protein . . . . 11 grams
Sodium . . . . 115 milligrams

POTATO CHOWDER

8 servings/serving size: 1 cup

*T*his is a creamy, low-fat version of a potato lover's favorite!

- ◆ 2 tsp olive oil
- ◆ 3/4 cup chopped onion
- ◆ 1/2 cup diced celery
- ◆ 1 bay leaf
- ◆ 1 clove garlic, minced
- ◆ 1/4 cup flour
- ◆ 1/4 cup evaporated skim milk
- ◆ 2 cups skim milk
- ◆ 3-1/2 cups low-sodium chicken broth

- ◆ 1-1/2 lb potatoes, peeled and cut into 2-inch cubes
- ◆ 1 tsp salt (optional)
- ◆ 1 tsp dried basil
- ◆ 1/4 tsp dried thyme
- ◆ 1/4 tsp nutmeg
- ◆ 1/4 tsp celery seeds
- ◆ Fresh ground pepper
- ◆ 1 Tbsp cider vinegar
- ◆ 1 Tbsp minced parsley

1. In a large saucepan, heat the oil. Add the onion, celery, and bay leaf; cook over medium heat for 5 minutes, stirring occasionally.
2. Add garlic and slowly add the flour; mix well. Slowly add the evaporated milk, skim milk, and chicken broth. Bring to a boil, stirring constantly.
3. Add the potatoes, salt, basil, thyme, nutmeg, celery seeds, and pepper. Reduce the heat and let simmer, uncovered, for 25 to 30 minutes or until potatoes are tender, stirring frequently.
4. Add the vinegar and discard the bay leaf. Remove 3 cups of the mixture and place in a food processor; puree. Add the mixture back to the soup pot and mix thoroughly. Sprinkle with parsley and serve.

....

Starch Exchange	1-1/2	Total Carbohydrate	23 grams
Calories	133	Dietary Fiber	2 grams
Total Fat	2 grams	Sugars	6 grams
Saturated Fat	0 grams	Protein	6 grams
Calories from Fat	19	Sodium	342 milligrams
Cholesterol	2 milligrams	w/o added salt	75 milligrams

QUICK MANHATTAN CLAM CHOWDER

8 servings/serving size: about 1 cup

*T*ry serving this chunky chowder with hot sourdough bread.

- 3 medium carrots, peeled and chopped coarsely
- 3 large white or russet potatoes, peeled and chopped coarsely
- 4 celery stalks, chopped coarsely
- 2-1/2 cups minced clams, drained
- 2 cups canned tomatoes, slightly crushed
- 1 Tbsp imitation bacon bits (optional)
- 1/2 tsp dried thyme or 1 tsp minced fresh thyme
- Dash salt and pepper

Add all the ingredients to a large soup pot. Cover and let simmer for 1 to 2 hours. Serve hot.

....

Lean Meat Exchange	1	Total Carbohydrate	23 grams
Starch Exchange	1-1/2	Dietary Fiber	3 grams
Calories	161	Sugars	7 grams
Total Fat	1 gram	Protein	15 grams
Saturated Fat	0 grams	Sodium	233 milligrams
Calories from Fat	11	w/o bacon bits	218 milligrams
Cholesterol	33 milligrams		

QUICK SHRIMP GUMBO

4 servings/serving size: 3 oz shrimp with sauce and 1/4 cup rice

Serve this spicy gumbo with a fresh spinach salad and warm rolls.

- ◆ 2 cups canned tomatoes, undrained
- ◆ 1/4 cup chopped green pepper
- ◆ 1 medium onion, chopped
- ◆ 1 cup uncooked white rice
- ◆ 1/2 cup low-sodium chicken broth

- ◆ 1 medium garlic clove, minced
- ◆ Dash hot pepper sauce
- ◆ Fresh ground pepper
- ◆ 12 oz precooked jumbo shrimp

1. Place all the ingredients except the shrimp in a large stockpot and bring to a boil. Reduce the heat, cover, and let simmer for 25 to 30 minutes.
2. Add the shrimp, cover, and simmer for 5 to 10 minutes or until shrimp is thoroughly heated. Serve hot.

....

Starch Exchange	1	Cholesterol	167 milligrams
Vegetable Exchange	1	Total Carbohydrate	21 grams
Lean Meat Exchange	1	Dietary Fiber	2 grams
Calories	182	Sugars	6 grams
Total Fat	2 grams	Protein	21 grams
Saturated Fat	0 grams	Sodium	396 milligrams
Calories from Fat	14		

SPANISH BLACK BEAN SOUP

6 servings/serving size: 1 cup

The combination of red wine and black beans gives this soup its robust flavor.

- 2 tsp chicken broth
- 1 tsp olive oil
- 3 garlic cloves, minced
- 1 yellow onion, minced
- 1 tsp minced fresh oregano
- 1 tsp cumin
- 1 tsp chili powder or 1/2 tsp cayenne pepper

- 1 red pepper, chopped
- 1 carrot, coarsely chopped
- 3 cups cooked black beans
- 1-1/2 cups low-sodium chicken broth
- 1/2 cup dry red wine

1. In a large pot, heat the chicken broth and olive oil. Add the garlic and onions and saute for 3 minutes. Add the oregano, cumin, and chili powder; stir for another minute. Add the red pepper and carrot.
2. Puree 1-1/2 cups of the black beans in a blender or food processor. Add the pureed beans, remaining 1-1/2 cups whole black beans, chicken broth, and red wine to the stockpot. Simmer 1 hour. Taste before serving; add additional spices if you like.

....

Starch Exchange	2	
Calories	155	
Total Fat	2 grams	
Saturated Fat	0 grams	
Calories from Fat	15	
Cholesterol	0 milligrams	

Total Carbohydrate	26 grams
Dietary Fiber	6 grams
Sugars	6 grams
Protein	9 grams
Sodium	29 milligrams

SPICY TURKEY CHILI

6 servings/serving size: 1 cup

*T*his chili tastes great with fresh-baked corn muffins (see recipe, page 214).

- ◆ **2 onions, chopped**
- ◆ **2 garlic cloves, minced**
- ◆ **1/2 cup chopped green pepper**
- ◆ **1 Tbsp olive oil**
- ◆ **1 lb lean ground turkey breast meat** (the meat department at the supermarket will grind this up for you)
- ◆ **2 cups kidney or pinto beans**
- ◆ **2 cups canned tomatoes with liquid**
- ◆ **1 cup low-sodium chicken broth**
- ◆ **2 Tbsp chili powder**
- ◆ **2 tsp cumin**
- ◆ **Fresh ground pepper**

1. In a large saucepan, saute the onion, garlic, and green pepper in the oil for 10 minutes. Add the turkey and saute until the turkey is cooked, about 5 to 10 minutes. Drain any fat away.
2. Add the remaining ingredients, bring to a boil, lower the heat, and simmer uncovered for 30 minutes. Add additional chili powder if you like your chili extra spicy.

- -

Starch Exchange 1-1/2	Cholesterol . . . . 51 milligrams
Lean Meat Exchange 2	Total Carbohydrate . . . . 23 grams
Calories 220	Dietary Fiber . . . . 5 grams
Total Fat . . . . 4 grams	Sugars . . . . 5 grams
Saturated Fat . . . . 1 gram	Protein . . . . 25 grams
Calories from Fat 32	Sodium . . . . 175 milligrams

WHITE BEAN SOUP

6 servings/serving size: 1 cup

Use any variety of white bean for this spectacular soup.

- 1/4 cup chopped onion
- 1 garlic clove, minced
- 2 Tbsp olive oil
- 1/2 lb dried great northern beans, white navy beans, or cannellini beans

- 2 qt water
- 2 bay leaves
- 1 tsp dried basil
- Dash salt and pepper
- 2 medium scallions, chopped
- 2 Tbsp minced fresh parsley

1. In a large saucepan, saute the onion and garlic in the oil for 5 minutes. Add the beans, water, bay leaves, and basil; stir well. Bring mixture to a boil, reduce the heat, cover and let simmer.
2. Continue to cook the soup for 2 hours or until beans are tender. Add water (if necessary), salt, and pepper; mix well.
3. In a blender or food processor, puree the mixture. Return the soup back to the saucepan and serve hot. Garnish with scallions and parsley.

....

Starch Exchange 1-1/2	Cholesterol . . . . 0 milligrams
Fat Exchange 1/2	Total Carbohydrate . . . . 22 grams
Calories 157	Dietary Fiber . . . . 6 grams
Total Fat . . . . 5 grams	Sugars . . . . 2 grams
Saturated Fat . . . . 1 gram	Protein . . . . 8 grams
Calories from Fat 43	Sodium . . . . 28 milligrams

PASTA

BAKED MACARONI AND CHEESE

6 servings/serving size: 1 cup

*T*his version is creamy and oh, so comforting.

- ◆ **1 cup uncooked elbow macaroni**
- ◆ **2 egg substitute equivalents**
- ◆ **1 cup evaporated skim milk**
- ◆ **1 cup small curd low-fat cottage cheese**
- ◆ **1/4 cup shredded sharp Cheddar cheese**

- ◆ **Dash salt**
- ◆ **Fresh ground pepper**
- ◆ **1 Tbsp Dijon mustard**
- ◆ **1 Tbsp fine dried bread crumbs** (to further reduce sodium, see recipe, page 217, for homemade version)

1. Prepare macaroni according to package directions, omitting salt. Drain and set aside.
2. In a large mixing bowl, combine the remaining ingredients except the bread crumbs with the cooked macaroni.
3. Coat a 1-quart baking dish with cooking spray and spoon the mixture into the dish. Sprinkle the top with bread crumbs. Bake at 350 degrees for 1 hour and serve hot.

....

Starch Exchange	1-1/2	Cholesterol	10 milligrams
Lean Meat Exchange	1	Total Carbohydrate	21 grams
Calories	170	Dietary Fiber	0 grams
Total Fat	3 grams	Sugars	6 grams
Saturated Fat	2 grams	Protein	14 grams
Calories from Fat	26	Sodium	324 milligrams

BEEF STROGANOFF

8 servings/serving size: 3 oz meat plus 1/2 cup noodles

*T*his casserole is hearty, tasty, and never goes out of style.

- ♦ **4 Tbsp olive oil**
- ♦ **2 Tbsp minced onion**
- ♦ **2 lb lean sirloin steak, pounded and cut into 1-inch cubes**
- ♦ **1/2 lb fresh mushrooms, sliced**
- ♦ **Fresh ground pepper**
- ♦ **Dash nutmeg**
- ♦ **1 cup low-fat sour cream**
- ♦ **9 oz uncooked noodles**

1. In a large skillet over medium heat, heat the oil, add the onion and beef, and saute for 5 minutes. Add the mushrooms, pepper, and nutmeg.
2. Reduce the heat to low and add the sour cream, stirring constantly until well blended.
3. Cook noodles in boiling water for 9 to 10 minutes. Drain. Place noodles on a serving dish and place beef mixture on top. Serve.

....

Starch Exchange	2	Cholesterol	89 milligrams
Lean Meat Exchange	3	Total Carbohydrate	28 grams
Fat Exchange	1	Dietary Fiber	1 gram
Calories	369	Sugars	6 grams
Total Fat	14 grams	Protein	32 grams
Saturated Fat	4 grams	Sodium	100 milligrams
Calories from Fat	127		

CORKSCREW PASTA WITH SAGE AND PEPPERS

8 servings/serving size: 1 cup

*T*his dish is simple to prepare and pretty to serve.

- ◆ 2 Tbsp chicken broth
- ◆ 1 garlic clove, minced
- ◆ 1/2 cup chopped onion
- ◆ 1/2 each red, green, and yellow peppers, cut into thin strips
- ◆ 2 Tbsp chopped fresh sage
- ◆ 15 oz tomato puree
- ◆ 1 Tbsp tomato paste
- ◆ 2 Tbsp red wine
- ◆ 1 tsp crushed red pepper (optional)
- ◆ 1 lb cooked corkscrew pasta (or any other shaped pasta)

1. In a large skillet over medium heat, heat broth. Add garlic and onion and saute for 5 to 8 minutes. Add peppers and saute for another 7 minutes.
2. Add sage, tomato puree, tomato paste, red wine, and red pepper. Lower heat to a simmer and cook for 15 minutes.
3. Add cooked pasta and let stand for 5 minutes. Serve.

....

Starch Exchange	1	Cholesterol	0 milligrams
Vegetable Exchange	1	Total Carbohydrate	24 grams
Calories	115	Dietary Fiber	1 gram
Total Fat	1 gram	Sugars	4 grams
Saturated Fat	0 grams	Protein	4 grams
Calories from Fat	5	Sodium	231 milligrams

EGGPLANT LASAGNA

6 servings/serving size: about 1 cup

Layers of tender eggplant replace noodles in this hearty entree that can be made ahead and frozen.

- 1-3/4 cups chopped onion
- 2 medium garlic cloves, minced
- 16 oz whole tomatoes, undrained
- 1/4 cup tomato paste
- 2 Tbsp fresh chopped parsley
- 1 tsp oregano
- 1/2 tsp dried basil
- Fresh ground pepper
- 1 large eggplant, peeled and sliced into 1/4-inch slices
- 1 cup shredded nonfat mozzarella cheese
- 1 cup low-fat cottage cheese
- 4 Tbsp grated Parmesan cheese

1. Coat a large skillet with nonstick cooking spray. Add onion and garlic and saute over low heat until onion is tender, about 6 minutes.
2. Stir in undrained whole tomatoes, tomato paste, parsley, salt, oregano, basil, and pepper. Bring mixture to a boil. Reduce heat and simmer, uncovered, for 40 to 50 minutes, stirring occasionally.
3. To steam eggplant slices, place 1 inch of water in a large pot. Arrange eggplant slices on a steamer, cover pot, and steam until eggplant is tender, about 5 minutes. Do not overcook.
4. Combine mozzarella and cottage cheeses together and set aside.
5. Coat a 13x9x2-inch baking pan with cooking spray, and place half of the eggplant in the pan. Top eggplant with half of the sauce mixture and half of the cheese mixture, and sprinkle with Parmesan cheese. Repeat the steps in layers until all the ingredients are used.
6. Bake at 350 degrees for 30 to 35 minutes, and serve hot.

....

Starch Exchange 1	Cholesterol .... 19 milligrams
Vegetable Exchange 1	Total Carbohydrate .... 18 grams
Medium-Fat Meat Exchange 1	Dietary Fiber .... 3 grams
Calories 177	Sugars .... 11 grams
Total Fat .... 6 grams	Protein .... 15 grams
Saturated Fat .... 4 grams	Sodium .... 546 milligrams
Calories from Fat 54	

FETTUCINE VERDE WITH TOMATO SAUCE

2 servings/serving size: about 1 cup

You probably have these ingredients in your cupboard right now.

- ◆ 1/4 lb uncooked spinach fettucine
- ◆ 2/3 cup skim milk ricotta cheese
- ◆ 1/2 cup canned tomatoes
- ◆ 1 large garlic clove, minced
- ◆ 1 small onion, finely chopped
- ◆ 1/4 tsp dried oregano
- ◆ 1/2 tsp dried basil
- ◆ 1 Tbsp grated Parmesan cheese

1. Prepare the pasta according to package directions, drain, and rinse thoroughly.
2. Place the pasta in a 1-quart casserole dish, and spoon ricotta cheese in center of pasta. Cover and bake at 300 degrees for 8 to 10 minutes until ricotta is heated through.
3. In a small saucepan, combine the tomatoes with the remaining ingredients, bring to a boil, reduce the heat, and let simmer for 3 to 5 minutes or until onion is tender.
4. Remove pasta from oven, and spoon sauce around ricotta cheese. Sprinkle Parmesan cheese over all and serve.

....

Starch Exchange 3
Vegetable Exchange 1
Medium-Fat Meat Exchange 1
Fat Exchange 1
Calories 382
Total Fat . . . . 10 grams
  Saturated Fat . . . . 5 grams
  Calories from Fat 91

Cholesterol . . . . 82 milligrams
Total Carbohydrate . . . . 53 grams
  Dietary Fiber . . . . 5 grams
  Sugars . . . . 12 grams
Protein . . . . 20 grams
Sodium . . . . 292 milligrams

FETTUCINE WITH PEPPERS AND BROCCOLI

4 servings/serving size: 1 cup

*T*his light pasta entree is loaded with Vitamin C–rich vegetables.

- ◆ **2 Tbsp olive oil**
- ◆ **2 medium garlic cloves, minced**
- ◆ **2 large red bell peppers, halved, seeded, and cut into 1/2-inch strips**
- ◆ **8 oz uncooked fettucine**
- ◆ **1-1/2 lb fresh broccoli**
- ◆ **1/4 cup grated Parmesan cheese**

1. In a large skillet over medium heat, heat the olive oil. Add the garlic and saute for 1 minute. Add the peppers and continue sauteing for 3 to 5 minutes or until peppers are just tender, stirring occasionally. Remove from heat and set aside.
2. Prepare the fettucine according to package directions (without adding salt) and drain. Wash the broccoli and peel the tough stalks (if necessary). Steam broccoli for 5 to 6 minutes until it is bright green and retains some crispness. Remove from the heat and set aside.
3. In a large bowl, toss the fettucine with the peppers, and arrange the broccoli on top. Sprinkle with Parmesan cheese and serve.

. . . .

Starch Exchange	3	Cholesterol*	58 milligrams
Vegetable Exchange	2	Total Carbohydrate	51 grams
Fat Exchange	1-1/2	Dietary Fiber	7 grams
Calories	362	Sugars	6 grams
Total Fat	11 grams	Protein	15 grams
Saturated Fat	2 grams	Sodium	142 milligrams
Calories from Fat	102		

*If the fettucine is made without egg (some is, some isn't), the cholesterol count is zero.

GARLIC FETTUCINE

5 servings/serving size: 1 cup

*T*his is a great dish for garlic lovers!

- ◆ **2 Tbsp olive oil**
- ◆ **12 plum tomatoes, seeded and diced**
- ◆ **4 cloves garlic, minced**
- ◆ **1/4 tsp salt (optional)**
- ◆ **Fresh ground pepper**

- ◆ **1 tsp capers**
- ◆ **2 tsp chopped black olives**
- ◆ **6 oz uncooked fettucine**
- ◆ **1/4 cup chopped fresh basil**
- ◆ **Parsley sprigs for garnish**

1. In a large saucepan over medium heat, heat the oil. Add the tomatoes, garlic, salt, pepper, capers, and olives. Let simmer over low heat for 30 minutes, stirring occasionally.
2. Prepare the fettucine according to package directions (without adding salt) and drain. Transfer the fettucine to a serving bowl and spoon sauce and chopped basil on top. Garnish with parsley sprigs to serve.

....

Starch Exchange 2	Cholesterol* . . . . 32 milligrams
Vegetable Exchange 1	Total Carbohydrate . . . . 38 grams
Fat Exchange 1	Dietary Fiber . . . . 4 grams
Calories 240	Sugars . . . . 10 grams
Total Fat . . . . 8 grams	Protein . . . . 7 grams
Saturated Fat . . . . 1 gram	Sodium . . . . 147 milligrams
Calories from Fat 71	w/o added salt . . . . . . 51 milligrams

*If the fettucine is made without egg (some is, some isn't), the cholesterol count is zero.

LINGUINE WITH CLAM SAUCE

4 servings/serving size: 4 oz sauce with 1/2 cup linguine

*T*ry this good red clam sauce recipe with other types of pasta or over rice.

- ♦ 1/2 cup finely chopped onion
- ♦ 1/2 cup finely chopped celery
- ♦ 3 medium garlic cloves, minced
- ♦ 7-oz can clams, minced and drained, reserve juice
- ♦ 15-oz can whole tomatoes, undrained and chopped
- ♦ 1/2 tsp dried basil
- ♦ 1/4 tsp dried oregano
- ♦ 1/2 tsp hot pepper sauce
- ♦ 1/3 cup finely minced parsley
- ♦ 2 cups cooked linguine, hot

1. Coat a large saucepan with nonstick cooking spray; place over medium heat until hot. Saute the onion, celery, and garlic until tender.
2. Add reserved clam juice, tomatoes, basil, oregano, and hot pepper sauce to saucepan. Bring to a boil; reduce heat and let simmer, uncovered, for 35 minutes.
3. Stir in clams and parsley; let simmer for 15 to 20 minutes, or until heated through. Place linguine on a platter, spoon sauce over the pasta, and serve.

....

Starch Exchange	1-1/2	Cholesterol	15 milligrams
Vegetable Exchange	2	Total Carbohydrate	29 grams
Calories	170	Dietary Fiber	3 grams
Total Fat	1 gram	Sugars	7 grams
Saturated Fat	0 grams	Protein	11 grams
Calories from Fat	12	Sodium	287 milligrams

LINGUINE WITH GARLIC BROCCOLI SAUCE

8 servings/serving size: 1 cup

White wine adds a special touch to this pasta dish.

- ◆ 3 Tbsp olive oil
- ◆ 8 medium garlic cloves, minced
- ◆ Fresh ground pepper
- ◆ 1/4 cup dry white wine
- ◆ 1 tsp dried oregano
- ◆ 1 tsp dried basil
- ◆ 1/2 tsp dried thyme
- ◆ 2 cups broccoli florets
- ◆ 1 lb uncooked linguine
- ◆ 1/4 cup grated Parmesan cheese
- ◆ 2 Tbsp pine nuts, toasted

1. In a medium skillet over medium heat, heat the oil. Add the garlic and pepper, sauteing for 5 minutes. Add the wine and bring to a boil. Reduce the heat and simmer for 3 to 4 minutes. Add the oregano, basil, and thyme.
2. To a large pot of boiling water, add the broccoli florets and then turn off the heat. Immediately rinse the broccoli under cold running water to stop the cooking process. (This method of blanching helps the broccoli to retain its bright green color and crispness.) Add the broccoli to the wine sauce and heat 2 more minutes.
3. Prepare the linguine according to package directions (without adding salt) and drain. Transfer the linguine to a large serving bowl and pour the wine sauce over the top. Sprinkle with Parmesan cheese and pine nuts to serve.

....

Starch Exchange	3	Cholesterol	2 milligrams
Fat Exchange	1	Total Carbohydrate	45 grams
Calories	293	Dietary Fiber	2 grams
Total Fat	8 grams	Sugars	4 grams
Saturated Fat	1 gram	Protein	10 grams
Calories from Fat	73	Sodium	58 milligrams

PASTA WITH VEGETABLE CLAM SAUCE

8 servings/serving size: 1/2 cup pasta plus sauce

This recipe works best with a shaped pasta like rigatoni or shells, so the vegetables stick to the pasta.

- ◆ **5 medium cloves garlic, crushed**
- ◆ **2 Tbsp olive oil**
- ◆ **4 celery stalks, chopped**
- ◆ **2 small zucchini, thinly sliced**
- ◆ **4 scallions, chopped**
- ◆ **1/4 lb fresh mushrooms, sliced**
- ◆ **2 Tbsp chopped fresh parsley**

- ◆ **7 oz clams, undrained**
- ◆ **2 small tomatoes, chopped**
- ◆ **1/3 cup dry white wine**
- ◆ **2 Tbsp fresh lemon juice**
- ◆ **Fresh ground pepper**
- ◆ **1 lb cooked, shaped pasta**
- ◆ **Grated Parmesan cheese**

1. In a large skillet over medium heat, saute garlic in oil until lightly browned. Add celery, zucchini, scallions, mushrooms, and parsley; saute until vegetables are just tender (about 5 minutes).
2. Add clams with their juice, tomatoes, wine, lemon juice, and pepper; stir well. Let simmer, uncovered, for 4 to 5 minutes. Place cooked pasta on a serving platter. Remove sauce from heat and spoon over the pasta. Sprinkle with cheese and serve.

....

Starch Exchange	. . . .	1
Vegetable Exchange	. . . .	1
Fat Exchange	. . . .	1
Calories	. . . .	162
Total Fat	. . . .	5 grams
Saturated Fat	. . . .	1 gram
Calories from Fat	. . . .	42

Cholesterol	. . . .	10 milligrams
Total Carbohydrate	. . . .	22 grams
Dietary Fiber	. . . .	2 grams
Sugars	. . . .	5 grams
Protein	. . . .	8 grams
Sodium	. . . .	94 milligrams

RIGATONI WITH CHICKEN AND THREE-PEPPER SAUCE

*8 servings/serving size: 1/2 chicken breast and
1 cup pasta with pepper sauce*

This dish is slightly spicy and very colorful!

- 16 oz uncooked rigatoni (or substitute any other shaped pasta)
- 1/4 cup olive oil
- 1 medium onion, chopped
- 1 large green pepper, julienned
- 1 large red pepper, julienned
- 1 large yellow pepper, julienned
- 2 garlic cloves, minced
- 2 tomatoes, chopped
- 1/2 cup low-sodium chicken broth
- 1/4 cup minced parsley
- 1/2 tsp dried basil
- Dash salt and pepper (optional)
- Dash crushed red pepper
- 2 Tbsp lemon juice
- 4 boneless, skinless chicken breasts, halved and cooked

1. Cook the rigatoni according to package directions (without adding salt), drain, and set aside. In a large skillet over medium heat, heat the oil. Add the onion, peppers, and garlic and saute for 6 minutes.
2. Add the tomatoes, chicken broth, parsley, basil, salt, pepper, and crushed red pepper. Add lemon juice. Add chicken to the skillet and cook chicken in sauce over low heat just until chicken is warmed in the sauce.
3. Arrange the cooked rigatoni on a serving platter. Spoon chicken and pepper sauce over rigatoni and serve.

....

Starch Exchange 3	Cholesterol .... 72 milligrams
Vegetable Exchange 1	Total Carbohydrate .... 50 grams
Lean Meat Exchange 3	Dietary Fiber .... 3 grams
Calories 448	Sugars .... 6 grams
Total Fat .... 11 grams	Protein .... 35 grams
Saturated Fat .... 2 grams	Sodium .... 94 milligrams
Calories from Fat 100	w/o added salt ...... 78 milligrams

SHRIMP AND PASTA

8 servings/serving size: 1 cup

Shells, shrimp, and a bit of Romano cheese make this salad tasty and festive.

- 1 lb uncooked shell macaroni
- 12 oz frozen baby shrimp
- 6 scallions, thinly sliced
- 3 small zucchini, sliced
- 10 cherry tomatoes, halved
- 1 Tbsp dried Italian seasoning
- 1 Tbsp minced fresh garlic
- Fresh ground pepper
- 1 Tbsp grated Romano cheese
- 1/4 cup olive oil
- 1/3 cup red wine vinegar
- 1 small head butter lettuce

1. Cook the shell macaroni in boiling water for 6 to 7 minutes, adding the frozen shrimp after 4 minutes. Drain.
2. In a large bowl, combine the macaroni, shrimp, scallions, zucchini, and tomatoes. Sprinkle with Italian seasoning, garlic, pepper, and cheese and mix well.
3. Drizzle the olive oil and vinegar on top and toss until well coated; refrigerate until chilled. To serve, line a clear glass bowl with lettuce leaves and spoon mixture into the bowl.

Starch Exchange 3
Medium-Fat Meat Exchange 1
Calories 329
Total Fat . . . . 9 grams
  Saturated Fat . . . . 1 gram
  Calories from Fat 77
Cholesterol . . . . 72 milligrams
Total Carbohydrate . . . . 47 grams
  Dietary Fiber . . . . 3 grams
  Sugars . . . . 5 grams
Protein . . . . 16 grams
Sodium . . . . 105 milligrams

SPAGHETTI PIE

4 servings/serving size: about 1 cup

This is a great way to use leftover spaghetti.

- ◆ **4 cups cooked spaghetti (about 1/2 lb dry)**
- ◆ **2 egg whites**
- ◆ **2 Tbsp skim milk**
- ◆ **1/4 cup grated fresh Parmesan cheese**
- ◆ **1 tsp dried oregano**
- ◆ **1 tsp dried basil**
- ◆ **1 tsp paprika**
- ◆ **1/2 tsp rosemary**

1. In a medium bowl, combine all ingredients and mix well.
2. Pour spaghetti mixture into an ovenproof nonstick round casserole dish or skillet and spread evenly.
3. Bake pie, uncovered, at 350 degrees until golden brown, about 20 minutes. Cut into wedges and serve.

....

Starch Exchange 3
Calories 232
Total Fat . . . . 3 grams
  Saturated Fat . . . . 1 gram
  Calories from Fat 23
Cholesterol . . . . 4 milligrams

Total Carbohydrate . . . . 40 grams
  Dietary Fiber . . . . 2 grams
  Sugars . . . . 2 grams
Protein . . . . 11 grams
Sodium . . . . 126 milligrams

SPAGHETTI WITH PESTO SAUCE

8 servings/serving size: 1 cup pasta plus sauce

*F*resh basil, garlic, cheese, and pine nuts turn everyday spaghetti into
something special.

- **3 cups fresh basil, stems removed**
- **3 garlic cloves, chopped**
- **1/4 cup olive oil**
- **3/4 cup pine nuts, toasted**
- **1/4 cup grated Parmesan cheese**
- **Fresh ground pepper**
- **1 lb cooked spaghetti, hot**

1. Wash and dry basil. Place basil in a blender or food processor with garlic, olive oil, pine nuts, cheese, and pepper; puree.
2. Transfer cooked spaghetti to a serving bowl. Add pesto and toss thoroughly to serve.

....

Starch Exchange	2-1/2	Cholesterol	2 milligrams
Fat Exchange	2-1/2	Total Carbohydrate	35 grams
Calories	313	Dietary Fiber	3 grams
Total Fat	16 grams	Sugars	2 grams
Saturated Fat	3 grams	Protein	10 grams
Calories from Fat	144	Sodium	50 milligrams

STUFFED MANICOTTI

4 servings/serving size: 2 stuffed manicotti

*Y*ou can also use the filling for a lasagna or stuffed shells.

- ◆ **2 Tbsp low-sodium chicken broth**
- ◆ **1/2 cup minced onion**
- ◆ **1/2 cup minced carrot**
- ◆ **1 garlic clove, minced**
- ◆ **1 cup low-fat ricotta cheese**
- ◆ **1 egg substitute equivalent**

- ◆ **2 Tbsp Parmesan cheese**
- ◆ **1 Tbsp chopped fresh basil**
- ◆ **8 large manicotti shells, cooked**
- ◆ **2 cups marinara sauce** (see recipe, page 30)

1. In a skillet over medium heat, heat broth. Add onion, carrot, and garlic and saute for 5 to 7 minutes, until onion is tender.
2. In a large bowl, combine vegetables with ricotta cheese, egg, Parmesan cheese, and basil. Mix well.
3. Stuff some of the mixture into each shell. Place stuffed manicotti shells in a large casserole dish. Pour marinara sauce on top, and let cook at 350 degrees for 20 minutes.

....

Starch Exchange 2-1/2	Cholesterol . . . . 27 milligrams
Vegetable Exchange 1	Total Carbohydrate . . . . 45 grams
Lean Meat Exchange 1	Dietary Fiber . . . . 3 grams
Calories 275	Sugars . . . . 8 grams
Total Fat . . . . 4 grams	Protein . . . . 18 grams
Saturated Fat . . . . 2 grams	Sodium . . . . 458 milligrams
Calories from Fat 34	

VEGETABLE LO MEIN

8 servings/serving size: 1 cup

Restaurant-style lo mein has far too much fat to be considered healthy, so make this lower-fat version instead.

- ◆ 1 cup plus 2 Tbsp low-sodium chicken broth
- ◆ 2 garlic cloves, minced
- ◆ 1/4 cup minced scallions
- ◆ 2 tsp grated fresh ginger
- ◆ 2 carrots, peeled and cut into 1/4-inch slices
- ◆ 3 celery stalks, cut on the diagonal into 1/4-inch slices
- ◆ 1/2 cup sliced mushrooms
- ◆ 1-1/2 cups broccoli florets
- ◆ 2 Tbsp dry sherry
- ◆ 1 Tbsp lite soy sauce
- ◆ 1 tsp sesame oil
- ◆ 1 Tbsp cornstarch
- ◆ 1/2 lb cooked thin spaghetti noodles

1. In a large skillet or wok, heat 2 Tbsp of broth. Add garlic, scallions, and ginger and stir-fry for 30 seconds.
2. Add carrots, celery, and mushrooms and stir-fry for 5 minutes. Add broccoli and 1/2 cup of broth, cover, and steam for 5 minutes.
3. In a small bowl, combine the remaining 1/2 cup of broth with sherry, soy sauce, and sesame oil. Add cornstarch and mix well.
4. Remove cover, and add cornstarch mixture. Cook for 1 minute more, until mixture thickens. Toss in cooked noodles and mix well. Serve.

....

Starch Exchange 1	Cholesterol .... 0 milligrams
Vegetable Exchange 1	Total Carbohydrate .... 17 grams
Calories 92	Dietary Fiber .... 3 grams
Total Fat .... 1 gram	Sugars .... 3 grams
Saturated Fat .... 0 grams	Protein .... 3 grams
Calories from Fat 11	Sodium .... 128 milligrams

POULTRY

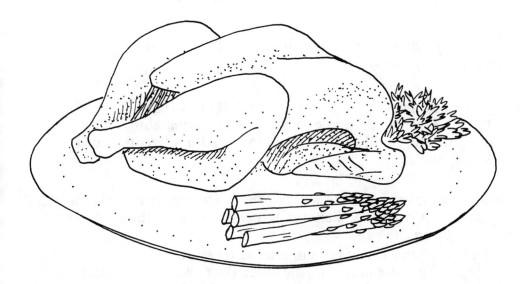

APPLE-GLAZED CORNISH HENS

8 servings/serving size: 4 oz

*T*his is a great dish to prepare during the holiday season as an alternative to turkey.

- ◆ **4 Cornish hens**
- ◆ **12 oz unsweetened apple juice concentrate, undiluted**
- ◆ **3 Tbsp water**
- ◆ **1 Tbsp cornstarch**
- ◆ **1 tsp cinnamon**
- ◆ **1 medium lemon, sliced**

1. Remove giblets from hens and discard. Rinse hens under cold water and pat dry. Using a long, sharp knife, split the hens lengthwise. You may also buy precut hens.
2. Place the hens, cavity side up, in a roasting pan. Dilute 1/2 cup of the apple juice concentrate with the water. Pour juice over the hens. Bake uncovered at 350 degrees for 45 minutes. Turn breast side up.
3. In a small pan over medium heat, combine the remaining apple juice concentrate, cornstarch, and cinnamon; mix well. Add 4 lemon slices and continue cooking until thickened.
4. Remove from heat and brush hens with the sauce. Return the hens to the oven and continue to bake for an additional 15 minutes. Transfer the hens to a serving platter and garnish with remaining lemon slices.

....

Fruit Exchange	1/2	Cholesterol	103 milligrams
Lean Meat Exchange	4	Total Carbohydrate	5 grams
Calories	241	Dietary Fiber	0 grams
Total Fat	9 grams	Sugars	4 grams
Saturated Fat	2 grams	Protein	34 grams
Calories from Fat	78	Sodium	106 milligrams

BAKED CHICKEN AND PEAS

4 servings/serving size: 4 oz chicken

Just add a salad, and you have dinner.

- ◆ 1 Tbsp olive oil
- ◆ 2 Tbsp lite soy sauce
- ◆ 1-1/2 tsp paprika
- ◆ 1/2 tsp basil
- ◆ 1/2 tsp thyme
- ◆ 4 chicken thighs, skinned

- ◆ 1/4 lb fresh mushrooms, sliced
- ◆ 1/2 cup low-sodium chicken broth
- ◆ 10 oz frozen peas, thawed and drained

1. In a shallow 2-quart casserole dish, combine oil, soy sauce, paprika, basil, and thyme. Add chicken thighs, and coat the chicken well.
2. Add mushrooms and chicken broth.
3. Cover and bake at 350 degrees for 50 minutes. Add peas; cover and continue baking for an additional 10 to 15 minutes or until peas are tender. Remove from oven and serve hot.

....

Starch Exchange	1	Cholesterol	65 milligrams
Lean Meat Exchange	3	Total Carbohydrate	15 grams
Calories	252	Dietary Fiber	5 grams
Total Fat	11 grams	Sugars	6 grams
Saturated Fat	2 grams	Protein	23 grams
Calories from Fat	98	Sodium	441 milligrams

BAKED CHICKEN BREASTS SUPREME

6 servings/serving size: 3 oz chicken

An especially nice dish that is slightly rich without the worry of excess fat. You'll need to start the night before.

- ◆ **3 whole boneless, skinless chicken breasts, halved**
- ◆ **2 cups low-fat sour cream**
- ◆ **1/4 cup lemon juice**
- ◆ **4 tsp Worcestershire sauce**
- ◆ **1 tsp celery salt**
- ◆ **2 tsp paprika**
- ◆ **1 garlic clove, minced**

- ◆ **Dash salt**
- ◆ **Fresh ground pepper**
- ◆ **1-3/4 cups dried bread crumbs** (see recipe, page 217)
- ◆ **1/4 cup olive oil**
- ◆ **Parsley sprigs**
- ◆ **1 lemon, sliced**

1. Wash chicken breasts under cold running water and pat dry. Combine sour cream, lemon juice, Worcestershire sauce, celery salt, paprika, garlic, salt, and pepper. Measure out 1/2 cup of marinade and reserve the rest in the refrigerator.
2. Add chicken to the 1/2 cup of marinade and coat each piece well. Refrigerate overnight. Remove chicken from the marinade, discard marinade, and roll chicken in bread crumbs, coating evenly.
3. Arrange in a single layer in a large baking pan. Drizzle olive oil over the chicken breasts. Bake the chicken at 350 degrees, uncovered, for 45 minutes.
4. Transfer to a serving platter, and serve with remaining marinade as a sauce and parsley and lemon slices as garnish.

··

Starch Exchange	1	Cholesterol	72 milligrams
Lean Meat Exchange	4	Total Carbohydrate	13 grams
Calories	312	Dietary Fiber	0 grams
Total Fat	15 grams	Sugars	6 grams
Saturated Fat	4 grams	Protein	30 grams
Calories from Fat	136	Sodium	282 milligrams

BAKED CHICKEN KIEV

6 servings/serving size: 3–4 oz

This low-fat version of a classic dish is great to serve when entertaining.

- ◆ **6 Tbsp low-calorie margarine**
- ◆ **3 Tbsp minced fresh parsley**
- ◆ **1/2 tsp dried rosemary**
- ◆ **1/4 tsp garlic powder**
- ◆ **Fresh ground pepper**

- ◆ **3 whole boneless, skinless chicken breasts, halved**
- ◆ **1/4 cup skim milk**
- ◆ **1/3 cup fine bread crumbs**
- ◆ **1 lemon, cut into wedges**

1. Combine margarine, parsley, rosemary, garlic, and pepper in a small mixing bowl. Shape margarine mixture into six 2-inch-long sticks; freeze until firm.
2. Place each chicken breast half between 2 sheets of waxed paper and flatten to 1/4 inch thickness with a meat mallet or rolling pin.
3. Place 1 margarine stick in the center of each chicken breast; fold ends over margarine and roll up, beginning with long side. Secure each end with wooden toothpicks.
4. Dip chicken rolls into the milk and coat thoroughly with bread crumbs. Bake at 400 degrees for 25 minutes until browned.
5. Arrange chicken on a serving platter, spoon juices from pan over the top, garnish with lemon wedges, and serve.

Lean Meat Exchange	4	Total Carbohydrate	5 grams
Calories	219	Dietary Fiber	0 grams
Total Fat	9 grams	Sugars	1 gram
Saturated Fat	2 grams	Protein	28 grams
Calories from Fat	81	Sodium	210 milligrams
Cholesterol	73 milligrams		

BAKED CHICKEN WITH WINE SAUCE

8 servings/serving size: 3–4 oz with sauce

*T*his wine sauce is also delicious with turkey or Cornish game hens.

- 4 Tbsp low-calorie margarine
- 4 whole boneless, skinless chicken breasts, halved
- 3 Tbsp flour
- 1/2 cup low-sodium chicken broth
- 3/4 cup low-fat sour cream
- 1/4 cup dry white wine

- 2 tsp grated lemon rind
- 1 tsp salt (optional)
- Fresh ground pepper
- 1 tsp minced fresh thyme
- 1/2 tsp ground sage
- 1/2 cup sliced mushrooms
- Fresh parsley sprigs

1. Melt 2 Tbsp of the margarine in a shallow baking dish; place chicken breasts in the dish. Bake in a 350-degree oven, uncovered, for 30 minutes.
2. Meanwhile, melt remaining margarine in a saucepan, add the flour, and stir until smooth. Add the chicken broth and stir until mixture is thickened. Add the sour cream, wine, lemon rind, salt, pepper, thyme, and sage. Stir until completely smooth.
3. Remove the chicken from the oven and turn the chicken breasts over. Cover the chicken with the mushrooms and pour the sauce over the top. Continue to bake, uncovered, for another 30 minutes or until chicken is tender. Transfer chicken to serving platter, spoon sauce over the chicken, garnish with parsley sprigs, and serve.

Starch Exchange	1/2	Cholesterol	72 milligrams
Lean Meat Exchange	3	Total Carbohydrate	6 grams
Calories	214	Dietary Fiber	0 grams
Total Fat	7 grams	Sugars	3 grams
Saturated Fat	2 grams	Protein	29 grams
Calories from Fat	67	Sodium	142 milligrams

BAKED LEMON CHICKEN

4 servings/serving size: 3 oz

This very light chicken dish is great on a spring or summer night.

- ◆ 3 Tbsp lemon juice
- ◆ 1 tsp fresh lemon zest
- ◆ 1 Tbsp finely chopped onion
- ◆ 1/4 tsp paprika
- ◆ 2 Tbsp olive oil

- ◆ Dash salt
- ◆ Fresh ground pepper
- ◆ 2 whole boneless, skinless chicken breasts, halved

1. In a small bowl, combine all ingredients except chicken.
2. Place chicken in a shallow baking dish and pour lemon mixture over it. Bake in a 400-degree oven for 45 minutes until chicken is tender.
3. Transfer chicken to a serving platter, spoon juices over it, and serve.

Lean Meat Exchange 3
Fat Exchange 1/2
Calories 205
Total Fat . . . . 10 grams
   Saturated Fat . . . . 2 grams
   Calories from Fat 88

Cholesterol . . . . 72 milligrams
Total Carbohydrate . . . . 1 gram
   Dietary Fiber . . . . 0 grams
   Sugars . . . . 0 grams
Protein . . . . 27 grams
Sodium . . . . 100 milligrams

CHICKEN AND SHRIMP

4 servings/serving size: 2–3 oz chicken and shrimp combined plus rice

*T*his skillet dinner cooks nicely while you prepare a salad and crusty bread.

- ◆ 1 Tbsp olive oil
- ◆ 2 medium onions, chopped
- ◆ 2 garlic cloves, minced
- ◆ 1 cup chopped celery
- ◆ 1 green pepper, chopped
- ◆ 2/3 cup uncooked rice
- ◆ 2 cups low-sodium chicken broth

- ◆ 1-1/2 cups cubed precooked chicken
- ◆ 16 oz stewed tomatoes
- ◆ 4 oz shrimp, shelled and deveined
- ◆ 1 tsp hot pepper sauce
- ◆ Fresh ground pepper

1. Coat a large skillet with the oil and heat over medium heat. Add onion, garlic, celery, and green pepper; saute until tender.
2. Stir in the rice, broth, chicken, and tomatoes. Bring to a boil, reduce the heat, and let simmer for 25 minutes. Add the shrimp, hot pepper sauce, and pepper and let simmer for 5 minutes. Transfer to a serving platter to serve.

....

Starch Exchange	. . . .	2-1/2
Vegetable Exchange	. . . .	1
Lean Meat Exchange	. . . .	2
Calories	. . . .	349
Total Fat	. . . .	9 grams
Saturated Fat	. . . .	2 grams
Calories from Fat	. . . .	79

Cholesterol	. . . .	80 milligrams
Total Carbohydrate	. . . .	43 grams
Dietary Fiber	. . . .	3 grams
Sugars	. . . .	13 grams
Protein	. . . .	25 grams
Sodium	. . . .	430 milligrams

CHICKEN AND ZUCCHINI

8 servings/serving size: 3–4 oz

*H*ere's *a quick stir-fry dish with a hint of ginger.*

- **1 Tbsp olive oil**
- **4 whole boneless, skinless chicken breasts, cut into thin strips about 1/8 inch wide**
- **2 garlic cloves, minced**
- **1 tsp grated fresh ginger**

- **1 Tbsp lite soy sauce**
- **1/3 cup sliced celery**
- **1/2 cup sliced fresh mushrooms**
- **1 cup julienned zucchini**
- **2 tsp cornstarch**
- **3 Tbsp water**

1. Heat the oil in a large skillet or wok. Add the chicken, garlic, and ginger. Stir-fry until chicken turns white, about 5 minutes. Stir in the soy sauce, celery, mushrooms, and zucchini.
2. Cover and continue to cook for about 5 minutes.
3. Add the cornstarch to the water and slowly add this mixture to the chicken, stirring constantly. Continue to cook for 2 to 5 minutes until mixture is thickened. Remove from heat and serve.

....

Lean Meat Exchange	3	Total Carbohydrate	2 grams
Calories	165	Dietary Fiber	0 grams
Total Fat	5 grams	Sugars	1 gram
Saturated Fat	1 gram	Protein	27 grams
Calories from Fat	43	Sodium	143 milligrams
Cholesterol	72 milligrams		

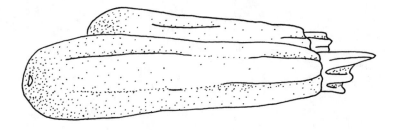

CHICKEN BURGERS

6 servings/serving size: 3–4 oz

*W*hen you tire of the same old hamburgers, try these for a delightful change.

- ◆ 1-1/4 lb ground chicken or turkey
- ◆ 1 egg substitute equivalent
- ◆ 1/4 tsp onion powder
- ◆ 1/4 tsp dried thyme
- ◆ 1/2 tsp poultry seasoning
- ◆ 1/4 tsp dried sage
- ◆ Dash salt
- ◆ Fresh ground pepper
- ◆ 6 Tbsp bread crumbs (see recipe, page 217)

1. In a medium bowl, combine all the ingredients except bread crumbs. Scoop meat into 6 patties and press each one lightly into the bread crumbs.
2. Prepare an outside grill or oven broiler and grill or broil 6 inches from heat for 4 to 5 minutes per side until cooked through. Serve warm on split buns and with your favorite condiments.

....

Starch Exchange	1/2	Cholesterol	48 milligrams
Lean Meat Exchange	3	Total Carbohydrate	5 grams
Calories	188	Dietary Fiber	0 grams
Total Fat	10 grams	Sugars	0 grams
Saturated Fat	3 grams	Protein	19 grams
Calories from Fat	88	Sodium	152 milligrams

CHICKEN DIJON

8 servings/serving size: 3–4 oz

Add colorful vegetables and wild rice for a complete meal.

- **4 whole boneless, skinless chicken breasts, halved**
- **1 Tbsp olive oil**
- **1/4 cup minced onion**
- **2 cups sliced fresh mushrooms**
- **2 garlic cloves, minced**
- **1/4 cup dry white wine**
- **1/2 cup low-sodium chicken broth**
- **4 Tbsp minced fresh parsley**
- **Fresh ground pepper**
- **1 Tbsp dijon mustard**

1. Place chicken breasts between 2 sheets of waxed paper; flatten to 1/4 inch using a meat mallet. Coat a large skillet with nonstick cooking spray and place over medium-high heat; heat until hot.
2. Add chicken to the skillet and cook for 2 to 3 minutes until chicken is browned on each side. Remove chicken from skillet; set aside and keep warm.
3. In the same pan, add the olive oil. Saute the onion, mushrooms, and garlic for 2 to 3 minutes. Add the wine, chicken broth, and 2 Tbsp of the parsley and cook for 3 to 4 minutes.
4. Add the chicken back to the pan and cook over medium heat for 10 to 12 minutes. Remove chicken and vegetables using a slotted spoon. Arrange the chicken on a serving platter and keep warm.
5. Continue cooking broth mixture until it is reduced to 1/3 cup. Remove from heat; whisk in the remaining parsley, pepper, and mustard. Spoon sauce over the chicken and serve.

....

Lean Meat Exchange 3
Calories 173
Total Fat . . . . 5 grams
   Saturated Fat . . . . 1 gram
   Calories from Fat 45
Cholesterol . . . . 72 milligrams

Total Carbohydrate . . . . 2 grams
   Dietary Fiber . . . . 1 gram
   Sugars . . . . 1 gram
Protein . . . . 27 grams
Sodium . . . . 93 milligrams

CHICKEN PAPRIKA

8 servings/serving size: 3 oz

This version of a classic Hungarian dish is much lower in fat.

- 1 Tbsp olive oil
- 1 large onion, minced
- 1 medium red pepper, julienned
- 1 cup sliced fresh mushrooms
- 1 cup water
- 1–2 tsp paprika
- 2 Tbsp lemon juice
- Dash salt
- Fresh ground pepper
- 4 whole boneless, skinless chicken breasts, halved
- 8 oz low-fat sour cream

1. Heat oil in a large skillet. Add onion, pepper, and mushrooms and saute until tender, about 3 to 4 minutes.
2. Add water, paprika, lemon juice, salt, and pepper, blending well. Add chicken; cover and let simmer for 25 to 30 minutes or until chicken is tender. Stir in the sour cream and continue to cook for 1 to 2 minutes. Do not boil. Serve hot.

....

Starch Exchange	. . . .	1/2
Vegetable Exchange	. . . .	1
Lean Meat Exchange	. . . .	3
Calories	. . . .	218
Total Fat	. . . .	7 grams
Saturated Fat	. . . .	2 grams
Calories from Fat	. . . .	62

Cholesterol	. . . .	72 milligrams
Total Carbohydrate	. . . .	9 grams
Dietary Fiber	. . . .	1 gram
Sugars	. . . .	6 grams
Protein	. . . .	29 grams
Sodium	. . . .	123 milligrams

CHICKEN PARMESAN

6 servings/serving size: 3 oz

Here's an all-time favorite that creates an enticing aroma.

- **3 whole boneless, skinless chicken breasts, halved**
- **1/2 cup bread crumbs** (to further reduce sodium, see recipe, page 217, for homemade version)
- **1/3 cup Parmesan cheese**
- **1 tsp dried oregano**
- **Fresh ground pepper**
- **2 egg substitute equivalents**
- **1/3 cup olive oil**
- **1 cup dry white wine**

1. Pound the chicken breasts until thin.
2. Combine the bread crumbs, Parmesan cheese, oregano, and pepper; set aside.
3. Beat the eggs in a shallow dish. Dip the chicken breasts into the egg and then the crumb mixture, coating both sides.
4. Heat the oil in a skillet, add chicken, and saute until golden brown, about 3 to 4 minutes on each side. Remove chicken and set aside on a platter.
5. Drain fat from the skillet and add the wine, bringing the mixture to a boil while scraping down residue from the skillet. Pour sauce over the chicken and serve.

....

Starch Exchange	1/2	
Lean Meat Exchange	4	
Fat Exchange	1/2	
Calories	304	
Total Fat	14 grams	
Saturated Fat	3 grams	
Calories from Fat	124	

Cholesterol	76 milligrams
Total Carbohydrate	7 grams
Dietary Fiber	0 grams
Sugars	1 gram
Protein	31 grams
Sodium	251 milligrams

CHICKEN PROVENÇAL

4 servings/serving size: 3–4 oz

Your guests will love this fast, easy-to-prepare dish.

- **2 Tbsp olive oil**
- **1 tsp dried basil**
- **2 whole boneless, skinless chicken breasts, halved**
- **1 medium garlic clove, minced**
- **1/4 cup minced onion**
- **1/4 cup minced green pepper**
- **1/2 cup dry white wine**
- **1 8-oz can tomatoes, chopped**
- **1/4 cup pitted black olives**
- **Fresh ground pepper**

1. Heat the oil in a skillet over medium heat. Stir in basil, add chicken, and brown about 3–5 minutes.
2. Add the remaining ingredients and cook uncovered over medium heat for 20 minutes or until chicken is tender. Transfer to serving platter and season with additional pepper before serving.

Vegetable Exchange 1
Lean Meat Exchange 4
Calories 240
Total Fat . . . . 11 grams
   Saturated Fat . . . . 2 grams
   Calories from Fat 98
Cholesterol . . . . 72 milligrams
Total Carbohydrate . . . . 5 grams
   Dietary Fiber . . . . 1 gram
   Sugars . . . . 4 grams
Protein . . . . 27 grams
Sodium . . . . 294 milligrams

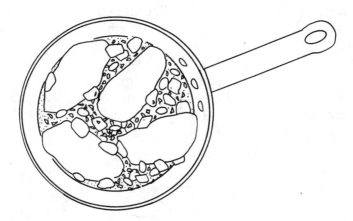

CHICKEN ROSE MARIE

6 servings/serving size: 3–4 oz

*T*ry serving this dish with orzo (a rice-shaped pasta) and good, crusty French bread.

- 3 whole boneless, skinless chicken breasts, halved
- 1 cup dried bread crumbs
- 1/4 cup olive oil
- 1/4 cup low-sodium chicken broth
- Grated zest of 1 lemon
- 3 medium garlic cloves, minced
- 1/4 cup minced fresh parsley
- 1/2 cup fresh lemon juice
- 1/2 cup water
- 1/2 tsp dried oregano
- 1 medium lemon, cut into wedges
- Parsley sprigs

1. Rinse the chicken in cold water and then roll it in bread crumbs. Spray a skillet with nonstick cooking spray and brown the coated chicken breasts over medium heat about 3 minutes on each side. Transfer the browned chicken to a baking dish.
2. In a small bowl, combine the remaining ingredients, except the lemon and parsley. Pour the sauce over the chicken. Bake the chicken at 325 degrees, uncovered, for 30 minutes until tender.
3. Transfer to a serving platter and spoon sauce over the chicken. Garnish with lemon and parsley.

Starch Exchange 1	Cholesterol . . . . 72 milligrams
Lean Meat Exchange 4	Total Carbohydrate . . . . 15 grams
Calories 300	Dietary Fiber . . . . 1 gram
Total Fat . . . . 13 grams	Sugars . . . . 3 grams
Saturated Fat . . . . 2 grams	Protein . . . . 29 grams
Calories from Fat 118	Sodium . . . . 225 milligrams

CHICKEN WITH ALMOND DUXELLES

8 servings/serving size: 3–4 oz

*T*ucked away inside these moist chicken breasts is a surprising, crunchy filling of almonds, mushrooms, and shallots.

- 1/4 cup olive oil
- 1/4 cup dry sherry
- 3/4 lb diced fresh mushrooms
- 4 medium shallots, finely minced
- 2 garlic cloves, minced
- 1 tsp minced fresh thyme
- Dash cayenne pepper
- 1/2 cup ground almonds
- Dash salt and pepper
- 4 whole boneless, skinless chicken breasts, halved
- Paprika
- 1/2 cup low-fat sour cream

1. In a large skillet over medium heat, heat the olive oil and sherry. Add the mushrooms, shallots, garlic, thyme, and cayenne pepper. Cook, stirring often, until mushrooms turn dark.
2. Add the ground almonds, salt, and pepper and saute for 2–3 minutes. Divide the mixture into 8 portions and place each portion in the center of each chicken breast half. Fold edges over, roll up, and place in a baking dish, seam side down, 1 inch apart.
3. Place about 1 Tbsp of sour cream over each chicken roll and sprinkle with paprika. Bake at 350 degrees for 25–30 minutes or until the chicken is tender. Transfer to a serving platter and serve.

....

Starch Exchange	1/2	Cholesterol .... 72 milligrams
Lean Meat Exchange	4	Total Carbohydrate .... 6 grams
Calories	262	Dietary Fiber .... 1 gram
Total Fat	13 grams	Sugars .... 5 grams
Saturated Fat	3 grams	Protein .... 29 grams
Calories from Fat	117	Sodium .... 101 milligrams

CHICKEN WITH CREAM SAUCE

4 servings/serving size: 3 oz

*T*his dish is good with steamed green beans or asparagus.

- **4 Tbsp olive oil**
- **2 whole boneless, skinless chicken breasts, halved**
- **3 Tbsp flour**
- **1/2 cup low-sodium chicken broth**
- **1 cup low-fat sour cream**
- **3/4 cup white wine**
- **2 tsp lemon zest**
- **1/2 tsp lemon pepper**
- **1/2 cup sliced mushrooms**
- **Parsley sprigs**

1. Place 2 Tbsp of oil in a shallow baking pan; place chicken breasts in oil and bake at 350 degrees for 15 minutes.
2. Place remaining 2 Tbsp of oil and flour in a saucepan and blend well. Add broth and continue stirring until mixture is smooth. Add sour cream, wine, lemon rind, and lemon pepper. Stir until well blended.
3. Remove chicken from oven and turn. Cover with mushrooms and pour sauce on top. Continue baking uncovered for 20 minutes or until tender. Transfer to a platter and garnish with parsley.

Starch Exchange 1	Cholesterol . . . . 72 milligrams
Medium-Fat Meat Exchange 4	Total Carbohydrate . . . . 13 grams
Calories 378	Dietary Fiber . . . . 0 grams
Total Fat . . . . 21 grams	Sugars . . . . 8 grams
Saturated Fat . . . . 5 grams	Protein . . . . 32 grams
Calories from Fat 187	Sodium . . . . 151 milligrams

CHICKEN WITH GREEN PEPPERCORN SAUCE

4 servings/serving size: 3–4 oz

This is a quick dish to fix when unexpected guests drop by.

- 2 Tbsp olive oil
- 2 whole boneless, skinless chicken breasts, halved
- 2 scallions, sliced
- 1 Tbsp flour
- 1/2 cup half-and-half
- 1/4 cup low-sodium chicken broth
- 1 tsp green peppercorns, drained
- 1/2 tsp salt (optional)
- 1/4 cup dry white wine

1. In a large skillet, heat the olive oil over medium heat. Saute chicken for 5 minutes per side; remove to a platter.
2. Saute scallions for 1 minute and add the flour. Add the half-and-half, chicken broth, peppercorns, and salt. Continue cooking until sauce thickens.
3. Stir in the wine and return the chicken to the pan. Continue cooking until chicken is cooked through. Transfer chicken to a platter and serve with sauce.

....

Lean Meat Exchange 4	Total Carbohydrate . . . . 3 grams
Fat Exchange 1/2	Dietary Fiber . . . . 0 grams
Calories 255	Sugars . . . . 2 grams
Total Fat . . . . 13 grams	Protein . . . . 28 grams
Saturated Fat . . . . 4 grams	Sodium . . . . 346 milligrams
Calories from Fat 120	w/o added salt . . . . . . 80 milligrams
Cholesterol . . . . 83 milligrams	

GRILLED CHICKEN WITH GARLIC

4 servings/serving size: 3–4 oz

*R*oasted garlic is the secret to this flavorful chicken dish.

- ◆ **2 whole boneless, skinless chicken breasts, halved**
- ◆ **2-1/2 cups red wine**
- ◆ **3 sprigs thyme**
- ◆ **10 garlic cloves, minced**
- ◆ **1/4 cup olive oil**
- ◆ **Fresh ground pepper**

1. In a medium baking dish, combine chicken, red wine, thyme, and half of the minced garlic. Marinate for 2 to 3 hours in the refrigerator.
2. Spread remaining cloves of garlic evenly across bottom of a small baking dish, cover with olive oil, and sprinkle with pepper. Bake garlic mixture in a 300-degree oven for 1-1/2 hours or until garlic is tender.
3. Place garlic mixture in a food processor or blender and puree. Remove chicken from marinade.
4. Grill chicken for 10 to 15 minutes, turning frequently and brushing with pureed garlic. Transfer to a platter and serve hot.

....

Lean Meat Exchange	4	Cholesterol	72 milligrams
Fat Exchange	1	Total Carbohydrate	2 grams
Calories	276	Dietary Fiber	0 grams
Total Fat	16 grams	Sugars	2 grams
Saturated Fat	3 grams	Protein	27 grams
Calories from Fat	149	Sodium	65 milligrams

GRILLED LEMON MUSTARD CHICKEN

6 servings/serving size: 3 oz

*N*ote *that you need to let the chicken marinate overnight in this recipe!*

- **Juice of 6 medium lemons**
- **1/2 cup mustard seeds**
- **1 Tbsp minced fresh tarragon**
- **2 Tbsp fresh ground pepper**
- **4 garlic cloves, minced**
- **2 Tbsp olive oil**
- **3 whole boneless, skinless chicken breasts, halved**

1. In a small mixing bowl, combine the lemon juice, mustard seeds, tarragon, pepper, garlic, and oil; mix well.
2. Place chicken in a baking dish and pour marinade on top. Cover and refrigerate overnight.
3. Grill chicken over medium heat for 10 to 15 minutes, basting with marinade. Serve hot.

Lean Meat Exchange 3	Total Carbohydrate . . . . 2 grams
Calories 167	Dietary Fiber . . . . 0 grams
Total Fat . . . . 5 grams	Sugars . . . . 2 grams
Saturated Fat . . . . 1 gram	Protein . . . . 27 grams
Calories from Fat 47	Sodium . . . . 69 milligrams
Cholesterol . . . . 72 milligrams	

HERBED CORNISH HENS

8 servings/serving size: 4 oz

A perfect blend of herbs and wine complement the natural flavor of Cornish game hens.

- ◆ 4 Cornish hens
- ◆ 2 cups light rosé wine
- ◆ 2 garlic cloves, minced
- ◆ 1/2 tsp onion powder
- ◆ 1/2 tsp celery seeds
- ◆ 1/2 tsp poultry seasoning
- ◆ 1/2 tsp paprika
- ◆ 1/2 tsp basil
- ◆ Fresh ground pepper

1. Remove the giblets from the hens; rinse under cold water and pat dry. Using a long, sharp knife, split each hen lengthwise. You may also buy precut hens.
2. Place the hens, cavity side up, on a rack in a shallow roasting pan. Pour 1-1/2 cups of the wine over the hens; set aside.
3. In a shallow bowl, combine the garlic, onion powder, celery seeds, poultry seasoning, paprika, basil, and pepper. Sprinkle half the combined seasonings over the cavity of each split half. Cover and refrigerate. Allow the hens to marinate for 2 to 3 hours.
4. Bake the hens uncovered at 350 degrees for 1 hour. Remove from oven, turn breast side up, pour remaining 1/2 cup wine over the top, and sprinkle with remaining seasonings.
5. Continue to bake for an additional 25 to 30 minutes, basting every 10 minutes until hens are done. Transfer to a serving platter and serve hot.

....

Lean Meat Exchange	4	Total Carbohydrate	0 grams
Calories	225	Dietary Fiber	0 grams
Total Fat	9 grams	Sugars	0 grams
Saturated Fat	2 grams	Protein	34 grams
Calories from Fat	78	Sodium	103 milligrams
Cholesterol	103 milligrams		

INDOOR BARBECUED TURKEY

10 servings/serving size: 3 oz meat

Have turkey anytime! This is slowly roasted turkey breast in a beer-mustard sauce.

- 5-lb (including bone) turkey breast
- 1 Tbsp prepared mustard
- 1/2 cup light beer
- 1/4 cup red wine vinegar
- 3/4 cup ketchup
- 1 Tbsp no-added-salt tomato paste
- 1/2 cup spicy no-added-salt tomato juice (or spice up mild juice with several drops of hot pepper sauce)
- Fresh ground pepper

1. Spread turkey breast with mustard. Combine beer, vinegar, ketchup, tomato paste, and tomato juice in a small bowl.
2. Pour mixture over turkey, then sprinkle with pepper. Roast, covered, for 1-1/2 hours at 350 degrees. Remove cover and roast an additional 1 hour, basting occasionally. Transfer to a serving platter and serve.

....

Lean Meat Exchange 3
Calories 155
Total Fat . . . . 1 gram
   Saturated Fat . . . . 0 grams
   Calories from Fat 8
Cholesterol . . . . 92 milligrams

Total Carbohydrate . . . . 2 grams
   Dietary Fiber . . . . 0 grams
   Sugars . . . . 1 gram
Protein . . . . 33 grams
Sodium . . . . 148 milligrams

MARINATED CHICKEN KABOBS

4 servings/serving size: 3–4 oz

These kabobs are great to grill on a hot summer night.

- 4 tsp fresh lemon juice
- 1/2 tsp cayenne pepper
- Fresh ground pepper
- 1-inch piece of fresh ginger, peeled and minced
- 1 tsp curry powder
- 4 tsp olive oil
- 2 whole boneless, skinless chicken breasts, halved, cut into 1/4-inch strips

1. In a medium bowl, combine all ingredients except the chicken. Add the chicken and let marinate overnight in the refrigerator.
2. Thread the chicken onto metal or wooden skewers.
3. Grill over medium heat until chicken is cooked throughout, about 15 minutes. Transfer to a platter and serve.

....

Lean Meat Exchange 3
Calories 181
Total Fat . . . . 7 grams
  Saturated Fat . . . . 1 gram
  Calories from Fat 66
Cholesterol . . . . 72 milligrams

Total Carbohydrate . . . . 0 grams
  Dietary Fiber . . . . 0 grams
  Sugars . . . . 0 grams
Protein . . . . 26 grams
Sodium . . . . 64 milligrams

MUSHROOM CHICKEN

4 servings/serving size: 3 oz chicken and 1/2 cup rice

*T*his *great dish for leftover chicken is ready in less than 20 minutes.*

- **2 Tbsp olive oil**
- **1/2 cup sliced fresh mushrooms**
- **2-1/2 cups cubed precooked chicken**
- **1/4 cup flour**
- **Dash salt**
- **Fresh ground pepper**
- **1/4 cup white raisins**
- **1/3 cup sherry**
- **1 cup evaporated skimmed milk**
- **2 cups precooked rice, hot**
- **1/2 cup toasted slivered almonds**

1. In a large skillet, heat oil over medium heat. Add mushrooms and saute for 3 minutes.
2. Add chicken, flour, salt, and pepper. Add raisins and sherry and cook until sherry has been absorbed.
3. Add the milk and let simmer for 20 minutes. Arrange the rice on a serving platter, spoon chicken mixture over rice, top with slivered almonds, and serve.

....

Starch Exchange 3
Medium-Fat Meat Exchange 4
Calories 531
Total Fat . . . . 20 grams
   Saturated Fat . . . . 4 grams
   Calories from Fat 183
Cholesterol . . . . 80 milligrams
Total Carbohydrate . . . . 49 grams
   Dietary Fiber . . . . 3 grams
   Sugars . . . . 14 grams
Protein . . . . 37 grams
Sodium . . . . 191 milligrams

OVEN-BAKED CHICKEN TENDERS

4 servings/serving size: 3 oz

Kids will love these bite-sized morsels of crunchy chicken that are baked, not fried. Serve with Marinara Sauce (see recipe, page 30).

- **2 whole boneless, skinless chicken breasts, halved**
- **2 egg whites, beaten**
- **1/2 cup whole-wheat cracker crumbs**
- **1 tsp dried basil**
- **1/2 tsp dried oregano**
- **1/2 tsp dried thyme**
- **2 tsp fresh grated Parmesan cheese**
- **1 tsp paprika**

1. Cut each chicken breast into 2x1/2-inch strips.
2. Dip each strip into egg whites.
3. On a flat plate or in a plastic bag, combine cracker crumbs with spices and cheese. Add chicken strips, and coat with the crumb mixture.
4. On a nonstick cookie sheet, place chicken strips side by side in one layer. Bake at 350 degrees for 10 to 12 minutes until golden and crunchy.

....

Starch Exchange	1/2	Cholesterol	73 milligrams
Lean Meat Exchange	3	Total Carbohydrate	6 grams
Calories	197	Dietary Fiber	0 grams
Total Fat	5 grams	Sugars	0 grams
Saturated Fat	1 gram	Protein	29 grams
Calories from Fat	46	Sodium	181 milligrams

POACHED CHICKEN
WITH BAY LEAVES

8 servings/serving size: 3 oz

You'll love this poached chicken, surrounded by tender vegetables in a bay leaf–scented broth.

- 4 qt low-sodium chicken broth
- 2 cups dry white wine
- 4 large bay leaves
- 4 sprigs fresh thyme
- Dash salt and pepper
- 1 4-lb chicken, giblets removed, washed and patted dry
- 1/2 lb carrots, peeled and julienned
- 1/2 lb turnips, peeled and julienned
- 1/2 lb parsnips, peeled and julienned
- 4 small leeks, washed and trimmed

1. In a large soup pot, combine broth, wine, bay leaves, thyme, salt, and pepper. Let simmer over medium heat while you prepare the chicken.
2. Stuff the cavity with 1/3 each of the carrots, turnips, and parsnips; then truss. Add the stuffed chicken to the soup pot and poach, covered, over low heat for 30 minutes.
3. Add remaining vegetables with the leeks and continue to simmer for 25 to 30 minutes, or until juices run clear when the chicken is pierced with a fork.
4. Remove chicken and vegetables to a serving platter. Carve the chicken, remove the skin, and surround the sliced meat with poached vegetables to serve.

....

Lean Meat Exchange 3
Calories 226
Total Fat . . . . 7 grams
    Saturated Fat . . . . 2 grams
    Calories from Fat 62
Cholesterol . . . . 75 milligrams

Total Carbohydrate . . . . 13 grams
    Dietary Fiber . . . . 3 grams
    Sugars . . . . 6 grams
Protein . . . . 26 grams
Sodium . . . . 138 milligrams

SAUTED CHICKEN WITH ARTICHOKE HEARTS

6 servings/serving size: 3–4 oz chicken with topping

*F*resh tarragon is best with this chicken and artichoke flavor combination!

- 3 whole boneless, skinless chicken breasts, halved
- 1/2 cup low-sodium chicken broth
- 1/4 cup dry white wine
- 2 8-oz cans artichokes, packed in water, drained and quartered
- 1 medium onion, diced
- 1 medium green pepper, chopped
- 1 tsp minced fresh tarragon (or 1/2 tsp dried)
- 1/4 tsp white pepper
- 2 tsp cornstarch
- 1 Tbsp cold water
- 2 medium tomatoes, cut into wedges

1. Coat a large skillet with nonstick cooking spray; place over medium heat until hot. Add the chicken and saute until lightly browned, about 3 to 4 minutes per side.
2. Add the chicken broth, wine, artichokes, onion, green pepper, tarragon, and white pepper; stir well. Bring to a boil, cover, reduce heat, and let simmer for 10–15 minutes or until chicken and vegetables are tender.
3. Combine the cornstarch and water; add to chicken mixture along with the tomato wedges, stirring until mixture has thickened. Remove from the heat and serve.

....

Vegetable Exchange 1	Cholesterol . . . . 73 milligrams
Lean Meat Exchange 3	Total Carbohydrate . . . . 9 grams
Calories 186	Dietary Fiber . . . . 2 grams
Total Fat . . . . 4 grams	Sugars . . . . 3 grams
Saturated Fat . . . . 1 gram	Protein . . . . 29 grams
Calories from Fat 8	Sodium . . . . 250 milligrams

SPICY CHICKEN DRUMSTICKS

2 servings/serving size: 3 oz

*S*erve these as an appetizer on a hot summer day.

- **1/4 cup plain low-fat yogurt**
- **2 Tbsp hot pepper sauce**
- **4 chicken drumsticks, skinned**
- **1/4 cup bread crumbs** (to further reduce sodium, see recipe, page 217, for homemade version)

1. In a shallow dish, combine yogurt and hot pepper sauce, mixing well. Add drumsticks, turning to coat, cover, and marinate in the refrigerator for 2–4 hours.
2. Remove drumsticks from marinade, dredge in bread crumbs, and place in a baking dish. Bake at 350 degrees for 40–50 minutes. Transfer to a serving platter and serve.

Starch Exchange 1/2
Lean Meat Exchange 3
Calories 204
Total Fat . . . . 6 grams
    Saturated Fat . . . . 2 grams
    Calories from Fat 51
Cholesterol . . . . 76 milligrams
Total Carbohydrate . . . . 10 grams
    Dietary Fiber . . . . 1 gram
    Sugars . . . . 1 gram
Protein . . . . 26 grams
Sodium . . . . 221 milligrams

SUMMER CHICKEN KABOBS

4 servings/serving size: 3 oz chicken

You can also grill these kabobs in the fall, when squash is in season.

- **1/4 cup lime juice**
- **2 Tbsp olive oil**
- **1 Tbsp minced parsley**
- **1/2 tsp dried thyme**
- **1 garlic clove, minced**
- **Fresh ground pepper**
- **2 whole boneless, skinless chicken breasts, cubed**

- **1 small yellow squash, cut into 2-inch pieces**
- **1 small zucchini, cut into 1-inch pieces**
- **4 large cherry tomatoes**

1. In a shallow dish, combine lime juice, oil, parsley, thyme, garlic, and pepper; mix well.
2. Add chicken, yellow squash, and zucchini, tossing to coat. Cover and refrigerate for 2 hours.
3. Alternate chicken, squash, and zucchini onto each of the skewers. Grill 4 inches from heat for 10 minutes, turning frequently. Add cherry tomatoes to each skewer during the last 1 minute of cooking. Remove from heat and serve.

....

Vegetable Exchange	1	Cholesterol .... 72 milligrams
Lean Meat Exchange	3	Total Carbohydrate .... 4 grams
Calories	189	Dietary Fiber .... 1 gram
Total Fat	7 grams	Sugars .... 2 grams
Saturated Fat	1 gram	Protein .... 27 grams
Calories from Fat	59	Sodium .... 67 milligrams

BEEF, PORK, & LAMB

APPLE CINNAMON
PORK CHOPS

2 servings/serving size: 3 oz meat plus apples

This dish will remind you of a crisp fall evening.

- ◆ 1 Tbsp canola oil
- ◆ 1 large apple, sliced
- ◆ 1 tsp cinnamon
- ◆ 1/4 tsp nutmeg
- ◆ 2 pork chops (4 oz each), trimmed of fat

1. In a medium nonstick skillet, heat the canola oil. Add apple slices and saute until just tender. Sprinkle with cinnamon and nutmeg, remove from heat, and keep warm.
2. Place pork chops in skillet, and cook thoroughly. Remove pork chops from skillet, arrange on a serving platter, spoon apple slices on top, and serve.

....

Fruit Exchange 1	Cholesterol . . . . 69 milligrams
Medium-Fat Meat Exchange 3	Total Carbohydrate . . . . 19 grams
Fat Exchange 1/2	Dietary Fiber . . . . 3 grams
Calories 318	Sugars . . . . 16 grams
Total Fat . . . . 16 grams	Protein . . . . 25 grams
Saturated Fat . . . . 4 grams	Sodium . . . . 49 milligrams
Calories from Fat 140	

Good recipe to keep meat tender

BAKED STEAK WITH ✖✖
CREOLE SAUCE

4 servings/serving size: 3–4 oz

This spicy creole sauce helps to keep the steak tender and juicy.

- **2 tsp olive oil**
- **1/4 cup chopped onion**
- **1/4 cup chopped green pepper**
- **8 oz canned tomatoes**

- **1/2 tsp chili powder**
- **1/4 tsp celery seed**
- **1/2 tsp garlic powder**
- **1 lb lean boneless round steak**

1. In a large skillet over medium heat, heat the oil. Add the onions and green pepper and saute until onions are translucent (about 5 minutes).
2. Add the tomatoes and the seasonings; cover and let simmer over low heat for 20 to 25 minutes. This allows the flavors to blend.
3. Trim all visible fat off the steak. In a nonstick pan or a pan that has been sprayed with nonstick cooking spray, lightly brown the steak on each side. Transfer the steak to a 13x9x2-inch baking dish; pour the sauce over the steak and cover.
4. Bake at 350 degrees for 1-1/4 hours or until steak is tender. Remove from oven; slice steak and arrange on a serving platter. Spoon sauce over the steak and serve.

....

Vegetable Exchange	1	Cholesterol	66 milligrams
Lean Meat Exchange	3	Total Carbohydrate	4 grams
Calories	195	Dietary Fiber	1 gram
Total Fat	9 grams	Sugars	2 grams
Saturated Fat	3 grams	Protein	24 grams
Calories from Fat	81	Sodium	150 milligrams

BEEF PROVENÇAL

4 servings/serving size: 4 oz

*F*resh zucchini and cherry tomatoes add color to this easy-to-make dish.

- ◆ 3 garlic cloves, minced
- ◆ 1 tsp dried basil
- ◆ Fresh ground pepper
- ◆ 4 lean beef cube steaks, 4 oz each

- ◆ 2 tsp olive oil
- ◆ 2 small zucchini, thinly sliced
- ◆ 6 cherry tomatoes, halved
- ◆ 3/4 cup grated Parmesan cheese

1. In a small bowl, combine the garlic, basil and pepper. Divide the mixture in half and rub one half of this mixture on both sides of the steaks. Reserve remaining seasonings.
2. In a large skillet over medium heat, heat the oil. Add the seasonings and heat for 30 seconds. Add the zucchini and saute for 3 minutes. Add the tomatoes and continue sauteing for 1 to 2 minutes. Remove from heat and transfer to a serving platter, sprinkle with cheese, and keep warm.
3. Add the steaks, 2 at a time, and pan-fry until desired degree of doneness; transfer to a platter. Spoon remaining juices over the steaks and serve them with the vegetables.

••

Vegetable Exchange 1	Cholesterol . . . . 91 milligrams
Lean Meat Exchange 4	Total Carbohydrate . . . . 5 grams
Fat Exchange 1/2	Dietary Fiber . . . . 1 gram
Calories 275	Sugars . . . . 3 grams
Total Fat . . . . 13 grams	Protein . . . . 33 grams
Saturated Fat . . . . 5 grams	Sodium . . . . 328 milligrams
Calories from Fat 120	

BEEF SHISH KABOBS

8 servings/serving size: 3 oz beef plus vegetables

While the kabobs are cooking, simmer some rice, and add a salad for a complete meal.

- 1/3 cup olive oil
- 1/4 cup red wine vinegar
- 1 Tbsp lite soy sauce
- 1 garlic clove, minced
- 1 Tbsp lemon juice
- Fresh ground pepper
- 2 lb lean beef, cubed

- 2 large bell peppers, red and green, cut into 1-inch pieces
- 1 lb mushrooms, stemmed
- 1 large tomato, cut into wedges
- 1 medium onion, quartered

1. Combine marinade ingredients (first 6 ingredients), and pour over the beef cubes. Let marinate 3 to 4 hours or overnight.
2. Place beef on skewers, alternating with peppers, mushroom caps, tomatoes, and onions. Grill over medium heat, turning and basting with marinade. Arrange skewers on a platter to serve.

....

Vegetable Exchange 2	Cholesterol . . . . 69 milligrams
Lean Meat Exchange 3	Total Carbohydrate . . . . 9 grams
Fat Exchange 1	Dietary Fiber . . . . 2 gram
Calories 262	Sugars . . . . 6 grams
Total Fat . . . . 13 grams	Protein . . . . 26 grams
Saturated Fat . . . . 3 grams	Sodium . . . . 112 milligrams
Calories from Fat 121	

BUTTERFLIED BEEF EYE ROAST

12 servings/serving size: 3–4 oz

*S*ince *this is a large piece of meat, be sure to let it marinate overnight or even for two days.*

- ◆ 3-lb lean beef eye roast, butterflied
- ◆ 3 Tbsp olive oil
- ◆ 1/4 cup water
- ◆ 1/2 cup red wine vinegar
- ◆ 3 garlic cloves, minced
- ◆ 1/2 tsp crushed red pepper
- ◆ 1 Tbsp chopped fresh thyme

1. Slice the roast down the middle, open it, and lay it flat in a shallow baking dish. In a small bowl combine the remaining ingredients and pour the mixture over the roast. Cover and let the meat marinate for at least 12 hours. Turn the roast occasionally.
2. Remove the roast from the marinade, discard the marinade, and place the roast on a rack in the broiler pan. Broil the roast 5 to 7 inches from the heat, turning occasionally, for 20 to 25 minutes or until desired degree of doneness.
3. Remove from oven, cover with foil, and let stand for 15 to 20 minutes before carving. Transfer to a serving platter, spoon any juices over the top, and serve.

··

Lean Meat Exchange 3	Total Carbohydrate . . . . 1 gram
Calories 168	Dietary Fiber . . . . 0 grams
Total Fat . . . . 7 grams	Sugars . . . . 1 gram
Saturated Fat . . . . 2 grams	Protein . . . . 24 grams
Calories from Fat 64	Sodium . . . . 51 milligrams
Cholesterol . . . . 57 milligrams	

HERBED POT ROAST

8 servings/serving size: 3 oz

*T*his lean roast simmers slowly in an herb marinade.

- 1 Tbsp olive oil
- 2-lb lean boneless beef roast
- Fresh ground pepper
- 1/2 cup water
- 1/3 cup dry sherry
- 1/4 cup ketchup
- 1 garlic clove, minced
- 1/4 tsp dry mustard

- 1/4 tsp marjoram
- 1/4 tsp dried rosemary
- 1/4 tsp dried thyme
- 2 medium onions, sliced
- 1 bay leaf
- 16 oz canned sliced mushrooms, undrained

1. Add olive oil to a large Dutch oven over medium heat. Sprinkle roast with pepper, and brown roast on all sides.
2. Combine water, sherry, ketchup, garlic, mustard, marjoram, rosemary, and thyme in a small bowl, and pour over roast. Add onions and bay leaf, cover, and simmer for 2 to 3 hours, until roast is tender.
3. Add mushrooms and continue simmering until heated. Remove bay leaf. Transfer roast to a platter, slice, and serve.

Starch Exchange	1/2	Cholesterol	87 milligrams
Lean Meat Exchange	3	Total Carbohydrate	7 grams
Fat Exchange	1/2	Dietary Fiber	1 gram
Calories	232	Sugars	3 grams
Total Fat	9 grams	Protein	29 grams
Saturated Fat	3 grams	Sodium	288 milligrams
Calories from Fat	82		

ITALIAN PORK CHOPS

4 servings/serving size: 1 pork chop with sauce

Serve this with fresh steamed broccoli and either flavored rice or shaped pasta.

- ◆ 4 lean pork chops (about 3–4 oz each)
- ◆ Fresh ground pepper
- ◆ 1/2 lb fresh mushrooms, sliced
- ◆ 1 medium onion, chopped
- ◆ 2 garlic cloves, crushed
- ◆ 2 medium green peppers, julienned

- ◆ 16 oz canned tomato sauce
- ◆ 1/4 cup dry sherry
- ◆ 1 Tbsp fresh lemon juice
- ◆ 1/4 tsp dried oregano
- ◆ 1/4 tsp dried basil

1. Trim all excess fat from the pork chops and sprinkle with pepper. Coat a large skillet with nonstick cooking spray, place chops in skillet, and brown on both sides.
2. Drain pork chops on paper towels and transfer to a 2-quart baking dish. Cover the chops with the mushrooms and set aside.
3. Saute the onions, garlic, and green peppers over medium heat until the onions are tender. Stir in the tomato sauce, sherry, lemon juice, oregano, and basil; let simmer, uncovered, for 10 to 15 minutes.
4. Pour tomato mixture over pork chops; cover and let bake at 350 degrees for 40 minutes or until pork chops are tender. Remove from oven and serve.

....

Starch Exchange	1	Cholesterol	77 milligrams
Vegetable Exchange	1	Total Carbohydrate	20 grams
Lean Meat Exchange	3	Dietary Fiber	3 grams
Calories	295	Sugars	8 grams
Total Fat	13 grams	Protein	27 grams
Saturated Fat	4 grams	Sodium	803 milligrams
Calories from Fat	113		

LAMB CHOPS WITH ORANGE SAUCE

Makes 4 servings/serving size: 2 lamb chops with sauce

*T*ry *serving these delicious orange-scented lamb chops with baby peas or French green beans.*

- ◆ 1/2 cup unsweetened orange juice
- ◆ 1 Tbsp orange rind
- ◆ 1/2 tsp dried thyme
- ◆ Fresh ground pepper
- ◆ 8 lean lamb chops, about 1/2 inch thick
- ◆ 1 Tbsp low-calorie margarine
- ◆ 1 cup sliced fresh mushrooms
- ◆ 1/2 cup dry white wine

1. In a shallow baking dish, combine the orange juice, orange rind, thyme, and pepper; mix well. Trim all excess fat from lamb chops and place in a baking dish. Spoon orange juice mixture over chops; cover and refrigerate for 3 to 4 hours, occasionally turning chops.
2. Coat a large skillet with nonstick cooking spray; place over medium-high heat until hot. Remove the chops from the marinade, reserving marinade; arrange in the skillet. Brown chops on both sides, remove from skillet, and drain.
3. Reduce heat to medium and melt margarine. Add mushrooms and saute until just tender. Stir in reserved marinade and wine and bring to a boil.
4. Return lamb chops to skillet; cover, reduce heat, and simmer for 10 to 12 minutes or until sauce is reduced to about 1/2 cup. Transfer lamb chops to platter, spoon orange sauce on top, and serve.

....

Starch Exchange 1/2	Cholesterol . . . . 72 milligrams
Lean Meat Exchange 3	Total Carbohydrate . . . . 5 grams
Calories 210	Dietary Fiber . . . . 1 gram
Total Fat . . . . 10 grams	Sugars . . . . 4 grams
Saturated Fat . . . . 3 grams	Protein . . . . 23 grams
Calories from Fat 86	Sodium . . . . 88 milligrams

LAMB KABOBS

6 servings/serving size: 1 kabob

*T*hese fresh, colorful kabobs are especially good served with wild rice.

- 1/2 cup low-calorie Italian salad dressing
- 1/4 cup fresh lemon juice
- 1 tsp dried oregano
- Fresh ground pepper
- 1-1/2 lb lean boneless lamb, cut into 2-inch pieces

- 1/2 lb mushrooms, stems removed
- 10 cherry tomatoes
- 1 red pepper, cut into 1-inch squares
- 1/2 yellow squash, cut into 1-inch chunks

1. In a shallow baking dish, combine the salad dressing, lemon juice, oregano, and pepper; mix thoroughly. Add lamb; cover, refrigerate, and let marinate for 6 hours or overnight.
2. Remove meat from marinade. Thread the lamb, alternating with vegetables, onto 6 skewers. Broil the skewers 7 to 8 inches from the heat for 18 to 20 minutes. Transfer to a platter and serve.

....

Vegetable Exchange	1	Cholesterol	76 milligrams
Lean Meat Exchange	3	Total Carbohydrate	6 grams
Calories	210	Dietary Fiber	2 grams
Total Fat	9 grams	Sugars	4 grams
Saturated Fat	3 grams	Protein	25 grams
Calories from Fat	84	Sodium	356 milligrams

MARINATED BEEF KABOBS

6 servings/serving size: 1 kabob

The marinade for this dish is quite tasty and easy to prepare. Try it with chicken, too.

- 1-1/2–lb lean sirloin steak, cut into 1-1/2–inch cubes
- 1 large red onion, cut into 1-inch cubes
- 1 each large green and red bell peppers, cut into 1-inch squares
- 1/2 lb mushrooms, stems removed
- 1/2 cup low-calorie Italian salad dressing
- 1/4 cup burgundy wine

1. Place cubed meat and prepared vegetables together in a shallow dish. In a small bowl, combine the salad dressing and wine; blend well. Pour the marinade over the meat and vegetables. Cover, refrigerate, and let marinate for at least 8 hours, stirring occasionally.
2. Alternate the meat and vegetables on 6 skewers. Grill kabobs over medium heat, turning often, for 15 to 20 minutes or until desired degree of doneness. Arrange on a platter and serve.

....

Vegetable Exchange	2	Cholesterol	74 milligrams
Lean Meat Exchange	3	Total Carbohydrate	11 grams
Calories	232	Dietary Fiber	2 grams
Total Fat	8 grams	Sugars	5 grams
Saturated Fat	3 grams	Protein	28 grams
Calories from Fat	75	Sodium	344 milligrams

MARINATED LEG OF LAMB

16 servings/serving size: 3-1/2–4 oz

Marinating one to two days is the secret to a great leg of lamb. Serve with steamed carrots and oven-roasted potatoes.

- 7-lb leg of lamb, boned and butterflied
- 3 cups dry red wine
- 1/4 cup olive oil
- 2 medium onions, sliced
- 1 large carrot, thinly sliced
- 6 parsley stems
- 2 bay leaves, crumbled
- 2 medium cloves garlic, minced
- Dash salt (optional)
- Fresh ground pepper
- Fresh parsley sprigs

1. In a large ceramic, glass, or stainless steel dish (anything but plastic), combine all the ingredients except the parsley sprigs; cover, refrigerate, and let marinate for 1 to 2 days, turning occasionally.
2. After marinating, drain lamb and pat dry. Place lamb into a grill basket. Broil the lamb 3 to 4 inches from the heat for 15 to 20 minutes per side.
3. Transfer lamb to a cutting board and let cool slightly. Carve lamb diagonally; transfer to serving platter, garnish with parsley sprigs and serve.

....

Lean Meat Exchange 4	Total Carbohydrate . . . . 0 grams
Calories 203	Dietary Fiber . . . . 0 grams
Total Fat . . . . 9 grams	Sugars . . . . 0 grams
Saturated Fat . . . . 3 grams	Protein . . . . 27 grams
Calories from Fat 85	Sodium . . . . 76 milligrams
Cholesterol . . . . 86 milligrams	w/o added salt . . . . . 67 milligrams

MARVELOUS MEAT LOAF

8 servings/serving size: 3 oz

By making meat loaf with beef, veal, and pork, you get a flavor that is out of this world.

- ◆ **1 lb lean ground beef**
- ◆ **1/2 lb ground veal**
- ◆ **1/2 lb ground pork**
- ◆ **3/4 cup bread crumbs** (to further reduce sodium, see recipe, page 217, for homemade version)
- ◆ **1 cup skim milk**

- ◆ **1 egg substitute equivalent**
- ◆ **1 medium onion, chopped** (for variety, add 1/4 cup shredded carrot, 2 Tbsp chopped green pepper, and/or 1/4 cup sliced celery)
- ◆ **16 oz canned stewed tomatoes**

1. In a large bowl, combine all ingredients except tomatoes. Place into loaf pan, and pour tomatoes over the top.
2. Bake at 350 degrees for 1 hour. Remove from oven, drain fat, slice, and serve.

....

Starch Exchange	1	Cholesterol	82 milligrams
Lean Meat Exchange	4	Total Carbohydrate	15 grams
Calories	284	Dietary Fiber	1 gram
Total Fat	12 grams	Sugars	6 grams
Saturated Fat	5 grams	Protein	27 grams
Calories from Fat	111	Sodium	328 milligrams

PORK CHOPS MILANESE

4 servings/serving size: 1 pork chop (about 2 oz meat)

You will win rave reviews when you prepare these.

- **1 cup fresh bread crumbs** (see recipe, page 217)
- **1/2 cup grated Parmesan cheese**
- **1/2 cup flour**
- **2 egg substitute equivalents, slightly beaten**
- **4 pork chops (3–4 oz each)**
- **3 Tbsp low-calorie margarine**
- **1 large lemon, cut into wedges**

1. Combine bread crumbs and Parmesan cheese in a shallow bowl. Dip the pork chops in flour, then eggs, and dredge in bread crumb mixture.
2. Melt margarine in a large skillet. Add pork chops and brown on both sides. Reduce heat, cover, and simmer for 3 to 5 minutes. Remove cover, and cook 5 to 10 minutes more until pork is completely cooked.
3. Squeeze 2 or 3 lemon wedges over chops. Transfer to a serving platter, garnish with remaining lemon wedges, and serve.

....

Starch Exchange 1-1/2
Lean Meat Exchange 3
Fat Exchange 1
Calories 332
Total Fat . . . . 14 grams
   Saturated Fat . . . . 5 grams
   Calories from Fat 122
Cholesterol . . . . 54 milligrams
Total Carbohydrate . . . . 24 grams
   Dietary Fiber . . . . 1 gram
   Sugars . . . . 2 grams
Protein . . . . 26 grams
Sodium . . . . 515 milligrams

PORK CHOPS NIÇOISE

6 servings/serving size: 1 pork chop with topping and 1/3 cup cooked rice

This one-skillet dish is easy to make, but elegant to serve!

- 1 Tbsp olive oil
- 6 lean pork chops (3–4 oz each)
- 4 large tomatoes, chopped
- 2 garlic cloves, minced
- 1 large green pepper, chopped
- 1 tsp dried basil
- 1/2 cup whole black olives
- 2 cups cooked rice, hot

1. In a large skillet, heat oil over medium heat. Add pork chops and lightly brown on both sides.
2. Add the tomatoes, garlic, pepper, and basil; cover. Simmer for 25 to 30 minutes, turning pork chops once. Add the olives and continue to simmer over low heat for 7 to 10 minutes.
3. Arrange rice on serving platter, place pork chops over rice, spoon sauce over the top, and serve.

....

Starch Exchange	1-1/2	Cholesterol	51 milligrams
Medium-Fat Meat Exchange	2	Total Carbohydrate	25 grams
Calories	275	Dietary Fiber	3 grams
Total Fat	12 grams	Sugars	6 grams
Saturated Fat	3 grams	Protein	18 grams
Calories from Fat	105	Sodium	155 milligrams

ROAST BEEF WITH CARAWAY SEEDS

8 servings/serving size: 3 oz

*S*erve this hearty dish with cabbage and noodles.

- 3/4 cup chopped onion
- 1 Tbsp caraway seeds
- 2-lb lean boneless chuck roast
- 1 Tbsp olive oil
- 1/3 cup red wine vinegar
- 1 cup unsweetened apple juice
- 1 Tbsp minced parsley
- 1/2 cup water

1. In a small bowl, combine 1/4 cup onion and caraway seeds and press into roast.
2. In a medium saucepan, saute remaining onion in olive oil. Place roast in a roasting pan and add the sauted onion.
3. Add vinegar, apple juice, parsley, and water. Bake roast uncovered at 325 degrees for 1 to 1-1/2 hours, basting frequently. Transfer roast to a platter and slice.

....

Starch Exchange	1/2	Cholesterol	87 milligrams
Lean Meat Exchange	3	Total Carbohydrate	6 grams
Calories	224	Dietary Fiber	0 grams
Total Fat	9 grams	Sugars	5 grams
Saturated Fat	3 grams	Protein	28 grams
Calories from Fat	81	Sodium	59 milligrams

STEAK DIANE*

2 servings/serving size: one 5–6 oz steak

*T*his classic recipe makes any occasion special.

- ◆ **2 beef tenderloin fillets, 5–6 oz each**
- ◆ **1 Tbsp flour**
- ◆ **Dash salt (optional)**
- ◆ **Fresh ground pepper**
- ◆ **1/4 cup low-calorie margarine**
- ◆ **1 tsp Dijon mustard**

- ◆ **6 large mushrooms, sliced**
- ◆ **2 medium scallions, sliced**
- ◆ **2 tsp Worcestershire sauce**
- ◆ **1/4 cup cognac**
- ◆ **1/2 cup low-sodium beef broth**
- ◆ **2 Tbsp chopped parsley**

1. Pound steak with a meat mallet, then coat with a mixture of flour, salt, and pepper. In a large skillet, melt 1 Tbsp of the margarine over medium heat.
2. Brown meat quickly, about 1 minute on each side; transfer meat to a platter. Spread meat on both sides with mustard; set aside.
3. Melt remaining margarine in the skillet and saute the mushrooms and scallions over medium heat. Add the Worcestershire sauce and cognac and ignite with a long match. Let the flames subside, then add beef broth.
4. Return the steaks to the skillet; cook until desired doneness, turning only once. Remove from heat, transfer to a platter, garnish with parsley, and serve.

. . . .

Starch Exchange	1/2	Cholesterol	91 milligrams
Medium-Fat Meat Exchange	5	Total Carbohydrate	9 grams
Calories	415	Dietary Fiber	1 gram
Total Fat	26 grams	Sugars	3 grams
Saturated Fat	8 grams	Protein	32 grams
Calories from Fat	234	Sodium	346 milligrams

*This recipe is high in fat.

STEAK WITH BRANDIED ONIONS

4 servings/serving size: 2–3 oz steak with onions

*T*his classic steak is great with a baked potato and a green salad.

- ◆ **12-oz lean sirloin steak**
- ◆ **4 Tbsp low-calorie margarine**
- ◆ **1/2 tsp garlic powder**
- ◆ **4 medium onions, sliced**
- ◆ **1 Tbsp chopped fresh parsley**
- ◆ **Dash brandy**

1. Prepare the sirloin steak to your liking.
2. In a medium skillet, melt the margarine and add garlic. Add the onions and parsley, sauteing until onions are tender.
3. Add brandy and let simmer for 1 to 2 minutes. Transfer steak to platter, spoon brandied onions over the top, and serve.

....

Vegetable Exchange 2	Cholesterol . . . . 56 milligrams
Lean Meat Exchange 3	Total Carbohydrate . . . . 11 grams
Fat Exchange 1/2	Dietary Fiber . . . . 2 grams
Calories 230	Sugars . . . . 7 grams
Total Fat . . . . 11 grams	Protein . . . . 21 grams
Saturated Fat . . . . 3 grams	Sodium . . . . 137 milligrams
Calories from Fat 102	

STIR-FRIED PORK TENDERLOINS

6 servings/serving size: 3 oz

The secret to this dish is not to overcook it.

- ◆ **1 lb pork tenderloins, cut into thin strips**
- ◆ **1 Tbsp vegetable oil**
- ◆ **1 Tbsp oyster sauce** (found in the Chinese food section of the grocery store)
- ◆ **1 Tbsp cornstarch**
- ◆ **1/2 cup low-sodium chicken broth**
- ◆ **1 Tbsp lite soy sauce**
- ◆ **1 cup fresh snow peas, trimmed**
- ◆ **1/2 cup sliced water chestnuts, drained**
- ◆ **1/2 cup minced red pepper**
- ◆ **1/4 cup sliced scallions**

1. In a large skillet or wok, heat oil. Stir-fry pork until strips are no longer pink.
2. Combine oyster sauce, cornstarch, chicken broth, and soy sauce in a measuring cup. Add to the pork and cook until sauce thickens.
3. Add vegetables, cover, and steam for 2 to 3 minutes. Serve.

Vegetable Exchange 1	Cholesterol . . . . 48 milligrams
Lean Meat Exchange 2	Total Carbohydrate . . . . 7 grams
Calories 155	Dietary Fiber . . . . 1 gram
Total Fat . . . . 6 grams	Sugars . . . . 3 grams
Saturated Fat . . . . 1 gram	Protein . . . . 18 grams
Calories from Fat 53	Sodium . . . . 151 milligrams

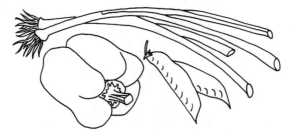

STUFFED BELL PEPPERS

4 servings/serving size: 1 pepper with sauce

Try using this basic filling to stuff zucchini or yellow squash, too.

- ◆ **4 medium peppers, red or green (or both)**
- ◆ **1 lb lean ground sirloin**
- ◆ **1 small onion, chopped**
- ◆ **1/3 cup instant white rice**
- ◆ **1 tsp dried oregano**
- ◆ **Dash salt**
- ◆ **Fresh ground pepper**
- ◆ **8 oz canned tomato sauce**
- ◆ **1/4 cup burgundy wine**
- ◆ **Grated Parmesan cheese to taste**

1. Slice off the stem end of each pepper and remove the seeds. In a medium bowl, combine the beef, onion, rice, oregano, salt, pepper, and 1/3 cup tomato sauce; mix well.
2. Stuff the mixture into the peppers and place them in a medium saucepan. Pour the wine and remaining tomato sauce over peppers.
3. Bring the peppers to a boil; cover and let simmer until they are tender, about 45 minutes. Add a few tablespoons of water if the sauce begins to cook away. Transfer to a serving platter, top with Parmesan cheese, and serve.

Starch Exchange	1/2	Cholesterol	71 milligrams
Vegetable Exchange	2	Total Carbohydrate	21 grams
Lean Meat Exchange	3	Dietary Fiber	2 grams
Calories	251	Sugars	6 grams
Total Fat	6 grams	Protein	28 grams
Saturated Fat	2 grams	Sodium	469 milligrams
Calories from Fat	54		

VEAL PICCATA WITH ORANGE SAUCE

4 servings/serving size: 3–4 oz

Fresh orange juice and sage make all the difference in this recipe—but they do need to be fresh!

- 1/2 cup flour
- Dash salt and pepper
- 6 Tbsp low-calorie margarine
- 1 lb lean veal cutlets

- 1 cup fresh orange juice
- 1 tsp minced fresh sage
- 1 orange, sliced
- 1 Tbsp minced fresh parsley

1. Place flour on a large plate and season with pepper and salt. In a large skillet, melt 4 Tbsp of margarine. Coat the veal with flour, shaking off excess. Add to the skillet, in batches, and cook for 30 seconds on each side. Transfer to a warm plate and keep warm.
2. Discard the pan drippings. Add 1/2 cup of the orange juice to the pan and bring to a boil, scraping up any browned bits. Boil for 1 to 2 minutes or until juice is reduced to a glaze.
3. Add remaining 1/2 cup orange juice and sage; season with salt and pepper and bring back to a boil. Boil for 1 to 2 minutes or until mixture thickens.
4. Remove from heat and whisk in remaining 2 Tbsp of margarine. Transfer veal to a platter, spoon orange sauce on top, and garnish with orange slices and fresh parsley to serve.

....

Starch Exchange	1	Cholesterol .... 117 milligrams
Lean Meat Exchange	4	Total Carbohydrate .... 18 grams
Calories	320	Dietary Fiber .... 1 gram
Total Fat	12 grams	Sugars .... 8 grams
Saturated Fat	3 grams	Protein .... 34 grams
Calories from Fat	106	Sodium .... 204 milligrams

VEAL ROMANO

6 servings/serving size: 3–4 oz

Y*ou can buy the roasted peppers for this dish in the condiment aisle of the supermarket (they come in jars) or in a gourmet deli.*

- **2 Tbsp olive oil**
- **1-1/2 lb lean veal cutlets**
- **1/4 cup flour**
- **Fresh ground pepper**
- **2 Tbsp low-calorie margarine**
- **1/2 cup dry white wine**

- **1/2 cup roasted red peppers, drained and julienned**
- **8 large black olives, thinly sliced**
- **2 Tbsp capers, rinsed and drained**

1. Heat the oil in a skillet over high heat. Place the cutlets between two pieces of waxed paper and pound with a meat mallet until they are about 1/4 inch thick.
2. Lightly flour the veal, shaking off the excess, and add to the skillet. Saute the veal for 2 to 3 minutes on each side, transfer to a platter, and sprinkle with pepper. Continue until all veal is cooked.
3. Melt the margarine in the skillet over high heat. Add the wine and scrape the brown bits from the skillet. Reduce heat to medium and add the peppers, olives, and capers, stirring occasionally.
4. Continue cooking until heated through. Spoon the sauce over the veal and serve.

....

Starch Exchange	1/2	Cholesterol .... 117 milligrams
Lean Meat Exchange	4	Total Carbohydrate .... 5 grams
Calories	270	Dietary Fiber .... 1 gram
Total Fat	12 grams	Sugars .... 1 gram
Saturated Fat	3 grams	Protein .... 33 grams
Calories from Fat	106	Sodium .... 189 milligrams

VEAL SCALLOPINI

4 servings/serving size: 3–4 oz

*S*erve this great dish with vermicelli and steamed broccoli or green beans.

- ◆ 4 lean veal cutlets (3–4 oz each)
- ◆ Fresh ground pepper
- ◆ 1 Tbsp olive oil
- ◆ 1/2 lb fresh mushrooms, sliced
- ◆ 1 large green pepper, cut into 1/2-inch strips
- ◆ 1/2 cup dry white wine
- ◆ 1/3 cup low-sodium chicken broth
- ◆ 1 Tbsp lemon juice
- ◆ 1 Tbsp cornstarch
- ◆ 2 Tbsp water
- ◆ 2 Tbsp minced fresh parsley

1. Place the veal cutlets between two pieces of waxed paper and pound until the cutlets are 1/8 inch thick. Sprinkle the veal with pepper and set aside.
2. Over medium heat, heat the oil in a large skillet. Add the veal, a few pieces at a time, cooking 2 to 3 minutes per side or until lightly browned. Remove from skillet and keep the veal warm while you prepare the sauce.
3. Saute the mushrooms and green pepper in the skillet for 3 minutes. Add the wine, broth, and lemon juice and bring to a boil. Dissolve the cornstarch with the water and add to the skillet, stirring constantly until mixture has thickened.
4. Remove from heat and stir in the parsley. Arrange the veal on a serving platter and pour the sauce over the top.

....

Vegetable Exchange	1	
Lean Meat Exchange	4	
Calories	252	
Total Fat	8 grams	
Saturated Fat	2 grams	
Calories from Fat	76	

Cholesterol	117 milligrams
Total Carbohydrate	7 grams
Dietary Fiber	1 gram
Sugars	2 grams
Protein	34 grams
Sodium	68 milligrams

SEAFOOD

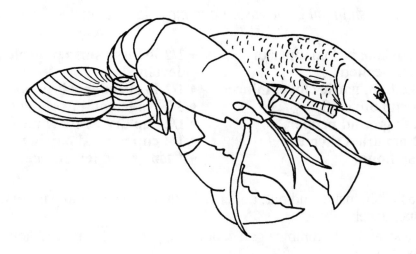

BAKED FISH IN FOIL

8 servings/serving size: 3 oz

*P*reparing fish in foil is the easiest and most flavorful method of cooking.

- ◆ 3-lb whole red snapper or bass, cleaned
- ◆ 1 medium garlic clove, minced
- ◆ 1/4 cup olive oil
- ◆ Fresh ground pepper
- ◆ 1/2 tsp dried thyme
- ◆ 1 tsp flour

- ◆ 1/2 lb large shrimp, peeled and deveined
- ◆ 1/2 lb sliced mushrooms
- ◆ 3 Tbsp lemon juice
- ◆ 1/2 cup dry white wine
- ◆ 1/4 cup minced parsley
- ◆ 1 tsp grated lemon peel

1. Wash fish, inside and out, under cold running water, and pat dry with paper towels.
2. In a small bowl, combine garlic, olive oil, pepper, thyme, and flour and mix well.
3. Place fish on a double thickness of heavy aluminum foil. In the cavity of the fish, place 1 Tbsp garlic mixture, 4 shrimp, and 1/2 cup sliced mushrooms. Sprinkle with 1 Tbsp lemon juice and 2 Tbsp wine.
4. Dot top of fish with remaining garlic mixture and arrange remaining shrimp and mushrooms on top. Sprinkle with remaining lemon juice and wine, parsley, and lemon peel.
5. Bring the long sides of the foil together over the fish and secure with a double fold. Fold both ends of foil upward several times.
6. Place fish on a cookie sheet; bake at 375 degrees for 30 to 35 minutes. Transfer to a serving platter and serve.

....

Lean Meat Exchange	3	Cholesterol	72 milligrams
Fat Exchange	1/2	Total Carbohydrate	2 grams
Calories	194	Dietary Fiber	1 gram
Total Fat	9 grams	Sugars	0 grams
Saturated Fat	1 gram	Protein	27 grams
Calories from Fat	77	Sodium	88 milligrams

BAKED GARLIC SCAMPI

4 servings/serving size: 3 oz

Scampi is always delicious served over a bed of rice. Remember to buy one pound of shrimp, total weight (with shells on).

- 1/3 cup low-calorie margarine
- Dash salt
- 7 garlic cloves, crushed
- 2 Tbsp chopped parsley
- 1 lb large shrimp, peeled, deveined, with tails left on
- 1 tsp grated lemon peel
- 1 Tbsp lemon juice

1. In a 13x9x2-inch baking pan, melt the margarine in a 400-degree oven. Add the salt, garlic, and 1 Tbsp parsley; mix well.
2. Arrange the shrimp in a single layer in the baking pan and bake at 350 degrees for 3 minutes, uncovered. Turn the shrimp and sprinkle with lemon peel, lemon juice, and the remaining 1 Tbsp parsley. Continue to bake 1 to 2 minutes more until the shrimp are bright pink and tender.
3. Remove shrimp from oven and arrange on a warm serving platter. Spoon garlic mixture over shrimp and serve.

....

Lean Meat Exchange	3	Total Carbohydrate	2 grams
Calories	166	Dietary Fiber	0 grams
Total Fat	8 grams	Sugars	2 grams
Saturated Fat	2 grams	Protein	20 grams
Calories from Fat	76	Sodium	331 milligrams
Cholesterol	180 milligrams		

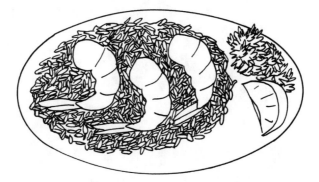

BAKED SHRIMP

4 servings/serving size: 3 oz (about 4 large shrimp)

Although great for every day, don't hesitate to prepare this for guests, too.

- ◆ **16 large shrimp**
- ◆ **2 Tbsp olive oil**
- ◆ **1–2 Tbsp water**
- ◆ **1/2 cup chopped parsley**
- ◆ **3 garlic cloves, minced**

- ◆ **1 cup bread crumbs** (to further reduce sodium, see recipe, page 217, for homemade version)
- ◆ **2 tsp paprika**
- ◆ **1 large lemon, cut into wedges**

1. With a small knife, cut down the back of the shrimp, but not all the way through, and flatten slightly. Place shrimp in a baking dish.
2. Combine olive oil, water, parsley, garlic, bread crumbs, and paprika. Mix thoroughly, and spoon mixture on each shrimp. Bake for 10 minutes at 400 degrees and garnish with lemon wedges.

....

Starch Exchange	1	Cholesterol	167 milligrams
Lean Meat Exchange	3	Total Carbohydrate	21 grams
Calories	255	Dietary Fiber	1 gram
Total Fat	9 grams	Sugars	2 grams
Saturated Fat	2 grams	Protein	22 grams
Calories from Fat	83	Sodium	426 milligrams

BAKED SHRIMP AND MUSHROOM CASSEROLE

8 servings/serving size: 2-1/2–3 oz

*These tender shrimp are covered with a light sherry cream sauce.
Remember to buy two pounds of shrimp, total weight (with shells on).*

- 6 Tbsp low-calorie margarine
- 1 lb mushrooms, sliced
- 2 Tbsp flour
- 1 tsp salt
- Fresh ground pepper
- 1/8 tsp nutmeg
- 1 cup half-and-half

- 2 lb shrimp, peeled, deveined, and boiled for 2 minutes
- 1/2 cup dry sherry
- 1/2 cup unsalted crackers, crushed
- 1 Tbsp chopped parsley

1. In a large skillet over medium heat, melt 4 Tbsp of the margarine. Add the mushrooms and saute for 3 to 5 minutes. With a slotted spoon, remove the mushrooms and arrange on the bottom of a 1-1/2–quart baking dish.
2. Whisk flour, salt, pepper, and nutmeg in the skillet until smooth. Gradually add the half-and-half and bring to a boil, stirring constantly. Reduce the heat and simmer for 1 to 2 minutes.
3. Add the shrimp and sherry, mixing well. Spoon the shrimp mixture over the mushrooms in the baking dish. Melt the remaining margarine and mix with the cracker crumbs. Sprinkle the cracker crumbs over the shrimp; sprinkle with parsley.
4. Bake uncovered at 350 degrees for 20 minutes or until the casserole is heated through and bubbly. Remove from the oven and serve hot.

....

Starch Exchange	1/2	Cholesterol	143 milligrams
Medium-Fat Meat Exchange	1	Total Carbohydrate	8 grams
Calories	188	Dietary Fiber	1 gram
Total Fat	9 grams	Sugars	2 grams
Saturated Fat	3 grams	Protein	17 grams
Calories from Fat	83	Sodium	534 milligrams

BASIC BOILED SHRIMP

6 servings/serving size: 4 oz

This is a good basic recipe to prepare shrimp for cocktail sauce.

- ◆ 4 bay leaves
- ◆ 20 peppercorns
- ◆ 12 whole cloves
- ◆ 1 tsp cayenne pepper
- ◆ 1 tsp dried marjoram
- ◆ 1/2 tsp dried basil
- ◆ 1/4 tsp dried thyme
- ◆ 1/8 tsp caraway seeds

- ◆ 1 tsp mustard seeds
- ◆ 1/8 tsp cumin seeds
- ◆ 1/4 tsp fennel seeds
- ◆ 8 cups water
- ◆ 1 large lemon, quartered
- ◆ 1 garlic clove, minced
- ◆ 2 lb large shrimp, peeled and deveined

1. In a double or triple thickness of cheesecloth, combine all the spices (first 11 ingredients). Secure the packet with a piece of string.
2. Combine water, lemon, garlic, and spice bag together in a Dutch oven. Bring the water to a boil, reduce the heat, and simmer for 3 minutes.
3. Add shrimp and return to a boil. Boil shrimp for 3 to 5 minutes. Drain thoroughly and chill. Serve with cocktail sauce.

....

Lean Meat Exchange	2	Total Carbohydrate	0 grams
Calories	113	Dietary Fiber	0 grams
Total Fat	1 gram	Sugars	0 grams
Saturated Fat	0 grams	Protein	24 grams
Calories from Fat	11	Sodium	255 milligrams
Cholesterol	222 milligrams		

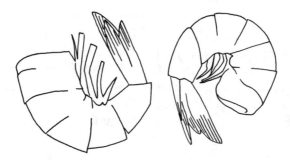

BROILED SOLE WITH MUSTARD SAUCE

6 servings/serving size: 3 oz with sauce

This delicious sauce keeps fish moist. Try it over cooked broccoli or string beans, too.

- ◆ 1-1/2 lb fresh sole fillets
- ◆ 3 Tbsp low-fat mayonnaise
- ◆ 2 Tbsp Dijon mustard
- ◆ 1 Tbsp chopped parsley
- ◆ Fresh ground pepper
- ◆ 1 large lemon, cut into wedges

1. Coat a baking sheet with nonstick cooking spray. Arrange fillets so they don't overlap.
2. In a small bowl, combine the mayonnaise, mustard, parsley, and pepper and mix thoroughly. Spread the mixture evenly over the fillets. Broil 3 to 4 inches from the heat for 4 minutes until fish flakes easily with a fork.
3. Arrange fillets on a serving platter, garnish with lemon wedges, and serve.

Lean Meat Exchange 2	Total Carbohydrate . . . . 1 gram
Calories 129	Dietary Fiber . . . . 0 grams
Total Fat . . . . 4 grams	Sugars . . . . 1 gram
Saturated Fat . . . . 1 gram	Protein . . . . 22 grams
Calories from Fat 34	Sodium . . . . 201 milligrams
Cholesterol . . . . 63 milligrams	

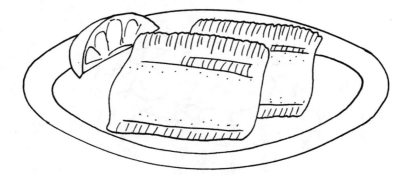

CRAB IMPERIAL

6 servings/serving size: 3 oz (1 custard cup)

This dish is suitable to serve as a light party luncheon entree or as an appetizer for dinner.

- ◆ **1 lb crabmeat, flaked**
- ◆ **1 egg substitute equivalent, slightly beaten**
- ◆ **1/2 cup low-fat mayonnaise**
- ◆ **2 Tbsp skim milk**
- ◆ **2 tsp capers**
- ◆ **Fresh ground pepper**
- ◆ **3 Tbsp grated Parmesan cheese**
- ◆ **1/4 cup chopped parsley**

1. Preheat the oven to 350 degrees. In a medium bowl, combine the crabmeat, egg, mayonnaise, milk, capers, and pepper. Stir until well blended.
2. Coat 6 custard cups with nonstick cooking spray and divide the mixture evenly into the cups. Sprinkle the tops with cheese and bake for 25 to 30 minutes.
3. Remove from the oven and garnish with chopped parsley before serving.

....

Medium-Fat Meat Exchange 2	Total Carbohydrate .... 2 grams
Calories 143	Dietary Fiber .... 0 grams
Total Fat .... 8 grams	Sugars .... 1 gram
Saturated Fat .... 2 grams	Protein .... 15 grams
Calories from Fat 72	Sodium .... 361 milligrams
Cholesterol .... 75 milligrams	

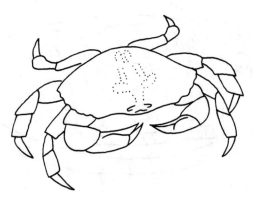

CRABMEAT STUFFING

8 servings/serving size: 4 oz

*U*se this stuffing to fill the cavity of a zucchini or yellow squash.

- 1/4 cup low-calorie margarine
- 1/4 cup flour
- 1 cup skim milk
- 1/2 Tbsp Worcestershire sauce
- 2 lb crabmeat, flaked

- 1/4 tsp nutmeg
- 1 Tbsp chopped red bell pepper
- 2 Tbsp minced parsley
- Dash salt
- Fresh ground pepper

1. Melt the margarine in a large skillet over medium heat; add flour and whisk until smooth.
2. Add the milk; continue cooking, stirring constantly, until thickened.
3. Add remaining ingredients; mix thoroughly. Continue to cook until crabmeat is heated through.

....

Starch Exchange 1/2	Cholesterol . . . . 97 milligrams
Lean Meat Exchange 2	Total Carbohydrate . . . . 5 grams
Calories 150	Dietary Fiber . . . . 0 grams
Total Fat . . . . 5 grams	Sugars . . . . 21 grams
Saturated Fat . . . . 1 gram	Protein . . . . 21 grams
Calories from Fat 41	Sodium . . . . 357 milligrams

FISH FILLETS WITH TOMATOES

4 servings/serving size: 3 oz

Use any white fish you like. This is good with orange roughy, flounder, sole, or perch.

- 1 medium tomato, minced
- 1 Tbsp minced onion
- 1/2 tsp fresh dill
- 1/4 tsp dried basil
- 1 lb fish fillets

- 2 Tbsp olive oil
- 1 Tbsp lemon juice
- 1/4 cup water
- 1 lemon, cut into wedges

1. Combine tomato, onion, dill, and basil.
2. Place fillets in a skillet and brush with the olive oil. Spoon tomato mixture over fish. Add lemon juice and water.
3. Simmer fillets over medium heat for 8 to 10 minutes. Transfer to a serving platter and garnish with lemon wedges.

....

Lean Meat Exchange 3	Total Carbohydrate . . . . 2 grams
Calories 167	Dietary Fiber . . . . 0 grams
Total Fat . . . . 8 grams	Sugars . . . . 1 gram
Saturated Fat . . . . 1 gram	Protein . . . . 21 grams
Calories from Fat 73	Sodium . . . . 94 milligrams
Cholesterol . . . . 58 milligrams	

FLOUNDER PARMESAN

4 servings/serving size: 3 oz

Instead of frying, why not have crusty baked fish?

- 1 lb flounder fillets
- 1/4 cup fresh grated Parmesan cheese
- 1 tsp dried oregano
- 1/4 tsp dried basil
- 1 Tbsp minced onion
- 1 tsp garlic powder
- 2 tsp paprika
- 2 Tbsp finely minced parsley
- Fresh ground pepper
- 8 oz low-fat sour cream

1. Place fish fillets in a baking dish.
2. Combine the remaining ingredients and spread over fish. Bake for 12 to 15 minutes at 375 degrees. Transfer to a platter and serve.

....

Starch Exchange 1/2	Cholesterol .... 61 milligrams
Lean Meat Exchange 3	Total Carbohydrate .... 8 grams
Calories 203	Dietary Fiber .... 0 grams
Total Fat .... 7 grams	Sugars .... 8 grams
Saturated Fat .... 3 grams	Protein .... 27 grams
Calories from Fat 60	Sodium .... 261 milligrams

FRESH FLOUNDER CREOLE

4 servings/serving size: 3 oz fish with creole sauce and garnish

Add a touch of New Orleans to dinner!

- 1 lb flounder fillets
- 3/4 cup chopped tomato
- 1/4 cup chopped green pepper
- 3 Tbsp fresh lemon juice
- 1-1/2 tsp olive oil
- 2 tsp hot pepper sauce

- 1 tsp finely chopped onion
- 1/2 tsp dried basil
- 1/2 tsp celery seed
- 1 large green pepper, sliced into rings
- 1 tomato, cut into wedges

1. Preheat the oven to 400 degrees. Spray a 13x9x2-inch baking dish with nonstick cooking spray; place fillets in the dish. In a medium bowl, combine all the ingredients except for the garnish; mix thoroughly.
2. Spoon creole mixture over fillets and bake for 10 minutes or until fish flakes easily with a fork. Transfer to a platter and garnish with pepper rings and tomato wedges to serve.

....

Vegetable Exchange 2	Cholesterol . . . . 59 milligrams
Lean Meat Exchange 2	Total Carbohydrate . . . . 9 grams
Calories 155	Dietary Fiber . . . . 2 grams
Total Fat . . . . 3 grams	Sugars . . . . 6 grams
Saturated Fat . . . . 1 gram	Protein . . . . 23 grams
Calories from Fat 30	Sodium . . . . 102 milligrams

GRILLED SALMON WITH DILL SAUCE

8 servings/serving size: 3–4 oz salmon with 2 Tbsp sauce

*P*erk up plain yogurt with the flavor of dill and moisten these grilled salmon steaks.

- ♦ 1 cup plain nonfat yogurt
- ♦ 2 tsp minced fresh dill
- ♦ 1/4 cup chopped scallions
- ♦ 1 tsp capers

- ♦ 2 tsp minced parsley
- ♦ 1 tsp minced chives
- ♦ 1 Tbsp olive oil
- ♦ 2 lb salmon steaks

1. In a small bowl, combine the first six ingredients and set aside. Spray the racks of your grill with nonstick cooking spray.
2. Brush the salmon steaks with olive oil and grill them over medium-hot coals for 4 minutes per side, or just until the salmon flakes with a fork.
3. Transfer the salmon to a platter and serve with dill sauce on the side.

Lean Meat Exchange 4	Total Carbohydrate . . . . 2 grams
Calories 218	Dietary Fiber . . . . 0 grams
Total Fat . . . . 11 grams	Sugars . . . . 2 grams
Saturated Fat . . . . 2 grams	Protein . . . . 26 grams
Calories from Fat 103	Sodium . . . . 81 milligrams
Cholesterol . . . . 79 milligrams	

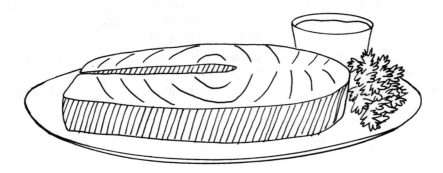

GRILLED SCALLOP KABOBS

6 servings/serving size: 1 kabob

Your guests will have fun preparing their own kabobs. If you're using wooden skewers, be sure to soak them in hot water for 15 minutes before you thread on the food. This will prevent the ends of the skewers from burning on the grill.

- 15 oz pineapple chunks, packed in their own juice, undrained
- 1/4 cup dry white wine
- 1/4 cup lite soy sauce
- 2 Tbsp minced parsley
- 1 tsp minced garlic
- Fresh ground pepper
- 1 lb scallops
- 18 large cherry tomatoes
- 1 large green pepper, cut into 1-inch squares
- 18 medium mushroom caps

1. Drain the pineapple, reserving the juice. In a shallow baking dish, combine the pineapple juice, wine, soy sauce, parsley, garlic, and pepper. Mix well.
2. Add the pineapple, scallops, tomatoes, peppers, and mushrooms. Marinate 30 minutes at room temperature, stirring occasionally.
3. Alternate pineapple, scallops, and vegetables on skewers. Grill the kabobs over medium-hot coals about 4 to 5 inches from the heat, turning frequently, for 5 to 7 minutes.

....

Vegetable Exchange 2	Cholesterol . . . . 26 milligrams
Lean Meat Exchange 1	Total Carbohydrate . . . . 13 grams
Calories 112	Dietary Fiber . . . . 3 grams
Total Fat . . . . 1 gram	Sugars . . . . 8 grams
Saturated Fat . . . . 0 grams	Protein . . . . 13 grams
Calories from Fat 11	Sodium . . . . 240 milligrams

GRILLED SHARK

4 servings/serving size: 3 oz

Because shark has flavor by itself, this recipe just brings out the natural flavor without a lot of complicated ingredients.

- ◆ **1 lb shark fillets**
- ◆ **3 Tbsp fresh lime juice**
- ◆ **Fresh ground pepper**
- ◆ **2 tsp olive oil**

- ◆ **1 Tbsp fresh chopped mint**
- ◆ **1 Tbsp fresh chopped cilantro**
- ◆ **1 garlic clove, minced**

1. Wash the shark fillets and combine with the lime juice. Sprinkle with pepper. Marinate refrigerated for 1 to 2 hours.
2. Combine oil, mint, cilantro, and garlic. Brush fillets with mixture. Grill over medium heat for 6 to 8 minutes, turning once. Transfer to a platter and serve.

....

Lean Meat Exchange	3	Total Carbohydrates	1 gram
Calories	161	Dietary Fiber	0 grams
Total Fat	7 grams	Sugars	1 gram
Saturated Fat	2 grams	Protein	23 grams
Calories from Fat	62	Sodium	103 milligrams
Cholesterol	44 milligrams		

GRILLED SWORDFISH WITH ROSEMARY

4 servings/serving size: 3 oz

When preparing swordfish, no need to fuss. Just a few touches here and there produces wonderful fish.

- ♦ **2 scallions, thinly sliced**
- ♦ **2 Tbsp olive oil**
- ♦ **2 Tbsp white wine vinegar**
- ♦ **1 tsp fresh rosemary**
- ♦ **4 swordfish steaks (3–4 oz each)**

1. Combine the marinade ingredients and pour over the swordfish steaks. Let marinate for 30 minutes.
2. Remove steaks from marinade, and grill for 5 to 7 minutes per side, brushing with marinade. Transfer to a serving platter and serve.

Lean Meat Exchange 3
Fat Exchange 1/2
Total Fat . . . . 11 grams
    Saturated Fat . . . . 2 grams
    Calories from Fat 101
Cholesterol . . . . 42 milligrams
Total Carbohydrate . . . . 0 grams
    Dietary Fiber . . . . 0 grams
    Sugars . . . . 0 grams
Protein . . . . 22 grams
Sodium . . . . 99 milligrams

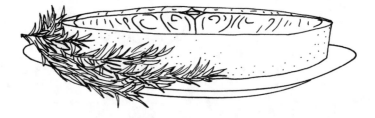

HALIBUT SUPREME

6 servings/serving size: 3 oz

This halibut has a crunchy almond topping.

- 1-1/2 lb halibut steaks
- 1 cup sliced mushrooms
- 1 Tbsp olive oil
- 1 small onion, finely chopped
- 3 Tbsp white wine
- 3/4 cup water
- Dash salt
- Fresh ground pepper
- 1/4 cup toasted almond slivers
- 1 Tbsp chopped parsley

1. Coat a 13x9x2-inch baking dish with cooking spray, and place halibut steaks in baking dish.
2. Add the remaining ingredients, except almonds and parsley, and bake at 325 degrees, basting frequently, for 25 minutes until fish flakes easily with a fork.
3. Remove from oven and top the halibut steaks with toasted almond slivers. Garnish with parsley.

....

Vegetable Exchange 1	Cholesterol . . . . 37 milligrams
Lean Meat Exchange 3	Total Carbohydrate . . . . 3 grams
Calories 186	Dietary Fiber . . . . 1 gram
Total Fat . . . . 7 grams	Sugars . . . . 2 grams
Saturated Fat . . . . 1 gram	Protein . . . . 25 grams
Calories from Fat 66	Sodium . . . . 85 milligrams

LOBSTER FRICASSEE

4 servings/serving size: 1/2 cup fricassee with 1/2 cup pasta or rice

A fricassee is traditionally served in a white sauce, but this low-fat version tastes just as good!

- ◆ **2 cups shelled lobster meat**
- ◆ **1/4 cup low-fat margarine**
- ◆ **3/4 lb mushrooms, sliced**
- ◆ **1/2 tsp onion powder**
- ◆ **1/2 cup skim milk**

- ◆ **1/4 cup flour**
- ◆ **1/4 tsp paprika**
- ◆ **Dash salt and pepper**
- ◆ **2 cups cooked rice or pasta**
- ◆ **Parsley sprigs**

1. Cut the lobster meat into bite-sized pieces. Melt the margarine in a sauce-pan; add the mushrooms and onion powder. Saute for 5 to 6 minutes.
2. Whisk the milk and flour in a small bowl, whisking quickly to eliminate any lumps. Pour milk mixture into mushroom mixture; mix thoroughly, and continue cooking for 3 to 5 minutes.
3. Add the lobster, paprika, salt, and pepper; continue cooking for 5 to 10 minutes until lobster is heated through.
4. Spread rice or pasta onto a serving platter, spoon lobster and sauce over the top, and garnish with parsley to serve.

....

Starch Exchange 2	Cholesterol . . . . 39 milligrams
Medium-Fat Meat Exchange 1	Total Carbohydrate . . . . 29 grams
Calories 244	Dietary Fiber . . . . 4 grams
Total Fat . . . . 6 grams	Sugars . . . . 4 grams
Saturated Fat . . . . 1 gram	Protein . . . . 17 grams
Calories from Fat 58	Sodium . . . . 349 milligrams

PAN-FRIED SCALLOPS

6 servings/serving size: 3–4 oz with 1/3 cup rice

Some people think scallops taste best when they are lightly pan-fried, which seals in all the natural juices.

- ◆ **1/2 cup fine dried bread crumbs**
- ◆ **1/4 tsp paprika**
- ◆ **Dash salt and pepper**
- ◆ **1-1/2 lb scallops**
- ◆ **1/4 cup olive oil**
- ◆ **1 Tbsp low-calorie margarine**
- ◆ **2 cups cooked rice, hot**
- ◆ **1/4 cup dry white wine**

1. Combine the bread crumbs, paprika, salt, and pepper in a small bowl. Roll the scallops thoroughly in the bread crumb mixture.
2. In a large skillet, heat the olive oil and margarine and saute the scallops quickly for about 2 to 3 minutes until lightly browned.
3. Spread the hot cooked rice on a serving platter and gently place the cooked scallops on top of the rice. Add the white wine to the remaining olive oil–margarine mixture in the pan. Bring to a slow boil. Remove from heat and pour over the rice and scallops to serve.

....

Starch Exchange 1-1/2	Cholesterol . . . . 39 milligrams
Medium-Fat Meat Exchange 2	Total Carbohydrate . . . . 22 grams
Calories 280	Dietary Fiber . . . . 1 gram
Total Fat . . . . 12 grams	Sugars . . . . 1 gram
Saturated Fat . . . . 2 grams	Protein . . . . 20 grams
Calories from Fat 104	Sodium . . . . 312 milligrams

POACHED RED SNAPPER

4 servings/serving size: 4 oz

*T*he whole fish is presented in this recipe. Have your fish store clean and scale the fish for you, but do leave on the head and tail.

- 1 cup dry white wine
- 1 medium lemon, sliced
- 6 parsley sprigs
- 5 peppercorns
- 5 scallions, sliced
- 2 bay leaves

- 1/2 tsp salt (optional)
- 1/2–1 cup water
- 1-1/2–2 lb dressed red snapper
- 1 lemon, sliced
- Parsley sprigs

1. In a fish poacher or very large skillet, combine the wine, lemon slices, parsley sprigs, peppercorns, scallions, bay leaves, salt, and water. Bring the mixture to a boil; add the snapper.
2. Cover the pan, lower the heat, and simmer the red snapper for 15 to 20 minutes until the fish flakes easily with a fork.
3. Carefully lift out the snapper and transfer to a platter. Garnish with lemon slices and parsley.

....

Lean Meat Exchange 2	Total Carbohydrate . . . . 0 grams
Calories 111	Dietary Fiber . . . . 0 grams
Total Fat . . . . 2 grams	Sugars . . . . 0 grams
Saturated Fat . . . . 0 grams	Protein . . . . 23 grams
Calories from Fat 14	Sodium . . . . 112 milligrams
Cholesterol . . . . 39 milligrams	w/o added salt . . . . . . 48 milligrams

SAUTED TROUT
ALMANDINE*

4 servings/serving size: 3 oz with topping

*P*an-dressed trout is gutted, but with the head and tail left on. Ask your fish market to do this for you.

- 1/2 cup flour
- 1/2 tsp salt (optional)
- Fresh ground pepper
- 4 pan-dressed trout (about 6–8 oz each)
- 1/3 cup olive oil

- 2 tsp low-calorie margarine
- 4 Tbsp chopped almonds
- 2 Tbsp fresh lemon juice
- 1 lemon, cut into wedges
- Parsley sprigs

1. In a plastic or paper bag, combine the flour, salt, and pepper. Place the trout in the bag one at a time and shake to coat.
2. Add 3 Tbsp of the olive oil to a large skillet and saute the trout over medium heat until golden brown on each side (about 4 to 5 minutes per side).
3. Remove the trout from the skillet and transfer to a warm serving platter. Keep warm. Add the remaining oil and margarine to skillet, add the almonds, and saute for 2 minutes. Add the lemon juice and cook a few minutes more.
4. Spoon the almonds over the trout and garnish with lemon wedges and parsley.

....

Starch Exchange	1	Cholesterol	63 milligrams
Medium-Fat Meat Exchange	3	Total Carbohydrate	14 grams
Fat Exchange	2-1/2	Dietary Fiber	1 gram
Calories	425	Sugars	2 grams
Total Fat	30 grams	Protein	26 grams
Saturated Fat	4 grams	Sodium	362 milligrams
Calories from Fat	266	w/o added salt	75 milligrams

*This recipe is high in fat.

SEA BASS WITH GINGER SAUCE

2 servings/serving size: 3–4 oz

Steaming fish is the healthiest way to prepare it—and it's always moist, never dried out.

- ♦ 2 sea bass fillets, 4 oz each
- ♦ 2 Tbsp peanut oil
- ♦ 2 Tbsp minced fresh ginger
- ♦ 2 garlic cloves, minced
- ♦ 1/3 cup minced scallions
- ♦ 4 tsp chopped cilantro
- ♦ 2 Tbsp lite soy sauce

1. In a medium steamer, add water and bring to a boil. Arrange the fillets on the steamer rack. Cover and steam for 6 to 8 minutes.
2. Meanwhile, heat the oil in a small skillet. Add the ginger and garlic and saute for 2 to 3 minutes.
3. Transfer the steamed fillets to a platter. Pour ginger oil over the fillets and top with scallions, cilantro, and soy sauce.

....

Vegetable Exchange	1	Cholesterol	45 milligrams
Medium-Fat Meat Exchange	3	Total Carbohydrate	3 grams
Calories	244	Dietary Fiber	0 grams
Total Fat	16 grams	Sugars	3 grams
Saturated Fat	3 grams	Protein	21 grams
Calories from Fat	145	Sodium	676 milligrams

SHRIMP CREOLE

4 servings/serving size: 2–3 oz shrimp with 1/2 cup cooked rice

This creole sauce is really versatile—you can add chicken cubes, lobster chunks, mussels, or clams instead of shrimp. Remember to buy one pound of shrimp, total weight (with shells on).

- 8 oz tomato sauce
- 1/2 cup sliced mushrooms
- 1/2 cup dry white wine
- 1/2 cup chopped onion
- 2 garlic cloves, minced
- 1/2 cup chopped green pepper
- 1/2 cup chopped celery
- 2 bay leaves
- 1/4 tsp cayenne pepper
- 1 lb shrimp, peeled and deveined
- 2 cups cooked rice, hot

1. In a large skillet, combine the tomato sauce, mushrooms, wine, onion, garlic, green pepper, celery, bay leaves, and cayenne pepper. Bring to a boil; cover, reduce the heat, and let simmer for 10 to 15 minutes.
2. Add the shrimp to the tomato sauce and cook uncovered for 3 to 5 minutes, until the shrimp are bright pink.
3. To serve, spread the rice on a platter, and spoon the shrimp and creole sauce over the rice.

....

Starch Exchange 2	Cholesterol .... 131 milligrams
Lean Meat Exchange 1	Total Carbohydrate .... 31 grams
Calories 213	Dietary Fiber .... 2 grams
Total Fat .... 1 gram	Sugars .... 4 grams
Saturated Fat .... 0 grams	Protein .... 18 grams
Calories from Fat 10	Sodium .... 534 milligrams

SHRIMP PROVENÇAL

8 servings/serving size: 2–3 oz shrimp with sauce

Serve crusty French bread to soak up this warm shallot and tomato sauce. Remember to buy two pounds of shrimp, total weight (with shells on).

- 2 Tbsp olive oil
- 1/4 cup chopped shallots
- 1 garlic clove, crushed
- 1 tomato, peeled and coarsely chopped
- 8 oz tomato sauce
- Dash salt and pepper
- Dash cayenne pepper
- 2 lb shrimp, shelled, deveined, and boiled for 5 minutes (until they just turn pink)
- 1/4 cup dry white wine
- 2 Tbsp chopped parsley

1. In a large skillet over medium heat, heat the oil. Saute the shallots and garlic for 2 minutes.
2. Add the chopped tomato, tomato sauce, salt, pepper, and cayenne pepper. Bring to a boil, stirring occasionally.
3. Reduce the heat to low and let simmer uncovered for 10 minutes. Stir in the shrimp and wine. Continue to cook for 5 minutes.
4. Remove from the heat and transfer to a serving platter. Sprinkle with parsley and serve.

....

Lean Meat Exchange	2	Total Carbohydrate	4 grams
Calories	117	Dietary Fiber	1 gram
Total Fat	4 grams	Sugars	2 grams
Saturated Fat	1 gram	Protein	15 grams
Calories from Fat	38	Sodium	354 milligrams
Cholesterol	131 milligrams		

VEGETABLE SALMON CAKES

4 servings/serving size: 4 oz

Canned salmon is an excellent source of calcium.

- 1 lb canned salmon, drained
- 1 cup dried bread crumbs
- 3 medium russet or white potatoes, skinned, cooked, and mashed
- 1/2 cup grated carrots
- 1/2 cup minced onion
- 2 Tbsp fresh lemon juice
- 2 egg substitute equivalents, slightly beaten

1. In a medium bowl, combine the salmon, 1/2 cup of the bread crumbs, potatoes, carrots, onion, lemon juice, and eggs, mixing well.
2. Coat a large skillet with nonstick cooking spray and place over medium heat. Form the salmon into patties and coat with remaining bread crumbs.
3. Place the salmon cakes in the heated skillet and cook for 6 minutes per side or until golden brown. Remove from heat, transfer to a serving platter, and serve hot.

....

Starch Exchange	2-1/2	Cholesterol	36 milligrams
Lean Meat Exchange	2	Total Carbohydrate	38 grams
Calories	322	Dietary Fiber	3 grams
Total Fat	7 grams	Sugars	4 grams
Saturated Fat	2 grams	Protein	27 grams
Calories from Fat	59	Sodium	729 milligrams

VEGETABLES

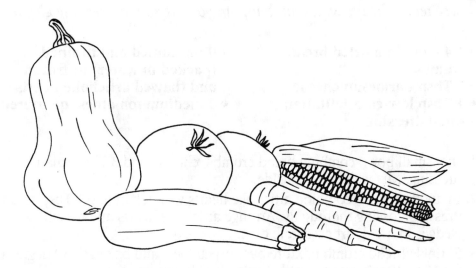

ARTICHOKES PARMESAN

4 servings/serving size: 1/2 cup

These tender hearts with crumb topping are as easy as they are elegant.

- 1/4 cup plain dried bread crumbs
- 2 Tbsp Parmesan cheese
- 4 Tbsp low-calorie Italian salad dressing
- 9 oz canned and drained (packed in water) or frozen and thawed artichoke hearts
- 2 medium tomatoes, quartered

1. In a small bowl, combine bread crumbs, cheese, and 3 Tbsp salad dressing. Mix well and set aside.
2. In another bowl, combine artichoke hearts with remaining 1 Tbsp salad dressing, tossing thoroughly. Arrange artichoke hearts and tomato wedges in a 1-quart casserole dish.
3. Sprinkle bread crumb mixture over vegetables, and bake at 350 degrees for 35 to 40 minutes or until topping is light brown.

....

Starch Exchange 1/2	Cholesterol . . . . 2 milligrams
Vegetable Exchange 1	Total Carbohydrate . . . . 14 grams
Fat Exchange 1/2	Dietary Fiber . . . . 12 grams
Calories 83	Sugars . . . . 8 grams
Total Fat . . . . 2 grams	Protein . . . . 4 grams
Saturated Fat . . . . 1 gram	Sodium . . . . 352 milligrams
Calories from Fat 18	

ASPARAGUS WITH VINAIGRETTE

6 servings/serving size: 1/2 cup

*T*he secret to great asparagus is to cook it until it is still bright green *and slightly crunchy. Look for thin asparagus with compact buds.*

- ◆ 1-1/2 lb fresh or frozen asparagus
- ◆ 1/2 cup red wine vinegar
- ◆ 1/2 tsp dried or 1 tsp fresh tarragon
- ◆ 2 Tbsp fresh chives
- ◆ 3 Tbsp fresh chopped parsley
- ◆ 1/2 cup water

- ◆ 1 Tbsp olive oil
- ◆ 2 Tbsp Dijon mustard
- ◆ 1 lb fresh spinach leaves, trimmed of stems, washed, and dried
- ◆ 2 large tomatoes, cut into wedges

1. Place 1 inch of water in a pot, and place steamer inside. Arrange asparagus on top of steamer. Steam fresh asparagus for 4 minutes and frozen asparagus for 6 to 8 minutes. Immediately rinse asparagus under cold water to stop the cooking. (This helps keep asparagus bright green and crunchy.) Set aside.
2. In a small bowl or salad cruet, combine remaining ingredients except spinach and tomatoes. Mix or shake well.
3. Pour dressing over asparagus and refrigerate for 5 to 6 hours.
4. To serve, line plates with spinach leaves, and place asparagus on top of spinach. Garnish with tomato wedges, and spoon any remaining dressing on top.

Vegetable Exchange 2	Cholesterol . . . . 0 milligrams
Fat Exchange 1/2	Total Carbohydrate . . . . 9 grams
Calories 68	Dietary Fiber . . . . 4 grams
Total Fat . . . . 3 grams	Sugars . . . . 4 grams
Saturated Fat . . . . 0 grams	Protein . . . . 4 grams
Calories from Fat 28	Sodium . . . . 127 milligrams

BROCCOLI WITH LEMON-BUTTER SAUCE

8 servings/serving size: 1/2 cup

*F*resh broccoli only needs a little enhancement.

- ◆ **1-1/2 lb fresh broccoli**
- ◆ **2 Tbsp unsalted butter**
- ◆ **2 Tbsp lemon juice**
- ◆ **1 large lemon, cut into wedges**

1. Wash broccoli, and trim tough stems. Cut each stalk of broccoli into several pieces.
2. Place broccoli into a vegetable steamer basket over boiling water. Cover and simmer for 10 minutes until broccoli is tender.
3. In a small skillet, melt butter, then add lemon juice. Drizzle lemon butter over broccoli, and serve with lemon wedges. Variation: for herbed broccoli, add 1/2 tsp marjoram and 1/2 tsp dried basil to the lemon-butter mixture.

....

Vegetable Exchange 1	Cholesterol . . . . 8 milligrams
Fat Exchange 1/2	Total Carbohydrate . . . . 4 grams
Calories 30	Dietary Fiber . . . . 2 grams
Total Fat . . . . 3 grams	Sugars . . . . 2 grams
Saturated Fat . . . . 2 grams	Protein . . . . 2 grams
Calories from Fat 30	Sodium . . . . 18 milligrams

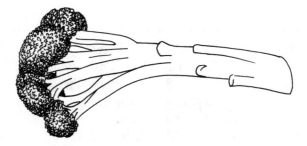

CARROTS MARSALA

6 servings/serving size: 1/2 cup

This side dish is so delicious you will want to serve this with an authentic Italian meal.

- **10 carrots (about 1 lb), peeled and diagonally sliced**
- **1/4 cup Marsala wine**
- **1/4 cup water**
- **1 Tbsp olive oil**
- **Fresh ground pepper**
- **1 Tbsp fresh chopped parsley**

1. In a large saucepan, combine carrots, wine, water, oil, and pepper. Bring to a boil, cover, reduce the heat, and simmer for 10 minutes, basting occasionally.
2. Transfer to a serving dish, spoon any juices on top, and sprinkle with parsley.

Vegetable Exchange 1	Cholesterol . . . . 0 milligrams
Fat Exchange 1/2	Total Carbohydrate . . . . 7 grams
Calories 53	Dietary Fiber . . . . 2 grams
Total Fat . . . . 2 grams	Sugars . . . . 3 grams
Saturated Fat . . . . 0 grams	Protein . . . . 1 grams
Calories from Fat 21	Sodium . . . . 39 milligrams

CHINESE ASPARAGUS

4 servings/serving size: 1/2 cup

This is a delicious complement to any Chinese meal.

- 1 lb asparagus
- 1/2 cup low-sodium chicken broth
- 2 Tbsp lite soy sauce
- 1 Tbsp rice vinegar

- 2 tsp cornstarch
- 1 Tbsp water
- 1 Tbsp canola oil
- 2 tsp grated ginger
- 1 scallion, minced

1. Trim the tough ends off the asparagus. Cut stalks diagonally into 2-inch pieces.
2. In a small bowl, combine broth, soy sauce, and rice vinegar.
3. In a measuring cup, combine cornstarch and water. Set aside.
4. Heat oil in a wok or skillet. Add ginger and scallions and stir-fry for 30 seconds. Add asparagus and stir-fry for a few seconds more. Add broth mixture and bring to a boil. Cover and simmer for 3 to 5 minutes until asparagus is tender.
5. Add cornstarch mixture and cook until thickened. Serve.

....

Vegetable Exchange 1	Cholesterol . . . . 0 milligrams
Fat Exchange 1	Total Carbohydrate . . . . 5 grams
Calories 60	Dietary Fiber . . . . 2 grams
Total Fat . . . . 4 grams	Sugars . . . . 2 grams
Saturated Fat . . . . 0 grams	Protein . . . . 2 grams
Calories from Fat 35	Sodium . . . . 313 milligrams

CREAMED SPINACH

4 servings/serving size: 1/2 cup

*T*his may become a family favorite!

- **1-1/2 lb fresh spinach leaves**
- **2 Tbsp low-calorie margarine**
- **2 Tbsp cornstarch**
- **Fresh ground pepper**
- **Dash salt**
- **3/4 cup evaporated skim milk**
- **1 egg substitute equivalent, beaten**

1. Remove and discard tough spinach stems. Wash leaves thoroughly and chop. Steam the spinach for 3 to 5 minutes and set aside.
2. In a skillet, heat margarine. Blend in cornstarch, pepper, and salt. Stir constantly.
3. Add milk, bring to a boil, and stir constantly for 1 minute. Remove sauce from heat.
4. Vigorously stir about 3 Tbsp sauce into the beaten egg and immediately add this mixture back to the skillet. Add steamed spinach to the skillet and coat with sauce. Serve.

....

Starch Exchange	1	Cholesterol	2 milligrams
Fat Exchange	1/2	Total Carbohydrate	13 grams
Calories	105	Dietary Fiber	2 grams
Total Fat	3 grams	Sugars	5 grams
Saturated Fat	1 gram	Protein	8 grams
Calories from Fat	28	Sodium	219 milligrams

CREOLE EGGPLANT

6 servings/serving size: 1/2 cup

*I*nstead of frying eggplant, dress it up in a tangy Creole sauce.

- 1 medium (4-oz) eggplant
- 2 medium garlic cloves, minced
- 1 large green bell pepper, chopped
- 1 medium onion, chopped
- 1/4 tsp dried thyme
- 1/4 tsp dried rosemary
- Dash hot pepper sauce (or to taste)
- 1/4 tsp chili powder
- 10 oz no-salt-added tomato sauce

1. Peel and cube eggplant. Place in a bowl of salted water (1/2 tsp) to cover, and let eggplant stand for 1 hour. Drain and pat dry.
2. Combine all ingredients in a large skillet over low heat, mixing well. Cover and simmer for 15 to 20 minutes until vegetables are tender. Transfer to a serving dish and serve.

· ·

Vegetable Exchange	2	Total Carbohydrate	10 grams
Calories	42	Dietary Fiber	2 grams
Total Fat	0 grams	Sugars	5 grams
Saturated Fat	0 grams	Protein	2 grams
Calories from Fat	0	Sodium	12 milligrams
Cholesterol	0 milligrams		

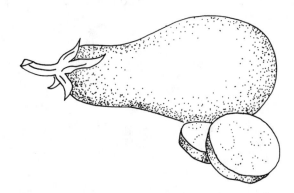

DILL-FLAVORED CARROTS

6 servings/serving size: 1/2 cup

You can eat these oven-baked carrots like French fries.

- **10 carrots (about 1 lb), peeled and cut into sticks similar to French fries**
- **1 Tbsp olive oil**

- **1/4 tsp dried dill weed**
- **Fresh pepper**
- **1 Tbsp water**

1. Place carrot sticks in the center of a large piece of aluminum foil. Add oil and sprinkle with dill weed, pepper, and water. Wrap carrots securely in foil, and crimp edges.
2. Bake at 375 degrees for 40 to 45 minutes or until carrots are tender.

. . . .

Vegetable Exchange 1
Fat Exchange 1/2
Calories 46
Total Fat . . . . 2 grams
   Saturated Fat . . . . 0 grams
   Calories from Fat 21

Cholesterol . . . . 0 milligrams
Total Carbohydrate . . . . 6 grams
   Dietary Fiber . . . . 2 grams
   Sugars . . . . 2 grams
Protein . . . . 1 gram
Sodium . . . . 38 milligrams

GREEN BEANS WITH GARLIC AND ONION

6 servings/serving size: 1/2 cup

This is a great side dish for Chinese food.

- ♦ 1 lb fresh green beans, trimmed and cut into 2-inch pieces
- ♦ 2 Tbsp olive oil
- ♦ 1 small onion, chopped
- ♦ 1 large garlic clove, minced
- ♦ 1/4 cup white vinegar
- ♦ 6 Tbsp grated Parmesan cheese
- ♦ Fresh ground pepper

1. Steam beans for 7 minutes or until just tender. Set aside.
2. In a skillet, heat oil over low heat. Add onion and garlic, and saute for 8 to 10 minutes or until onion is translucent. Transfer beans to a serving bowl and add onion mixture and vinegar, tossing well. Sprinkle with cheese and pepper and serve.

....

Vegetable Exchange	1	Cholesterol	4 milligrams
Fat Exchange	1-1/2	Total Carbohydrate	8 grams
Calories	97	Dietary Fiber	3 grams
Total Fat	6 grams	Sugars	2 grams
Saturated Fat	2 grams	Protein	4 grams
Calories from Fat	56	Sodium	96 milligrams

HERB-BROILED TOMATOES

4 servings/serving size: 1 tomato

These tomatoes are simple to fix, elegant to eat.

- **4 medium tomatoes**
- **1/4 cup grated Parmesan cheese**
- **2 Tbsp plain dried bread crumbs**
- **2 Tbsp fresh minced parsley**
- **1 tsp dried basil**
- **1 tsp dried oregano**
- **Fresh ground pepper**
- **1 Tbsp olive oil**

1. Remove stems from tomatoes, and cut in half crosswise. Combine remaining ingredients in a small bowl, and lightly press mixture over cut side of tomato halves.
2. Place tomatoes on a baking sheet, cut side up, and broil about 6 inches from the heat for 3 to 5 minutes or until topping is browned.

....

Vegetable Exchange 2
Fat Exchange 1
Calories 95
Total Fat . . . . 6 grams
   Saturated Fat . . . . 2 grams
   Calories from Fat 80
Cholesterol . . . . 4 milligrams
Total Carbohydrate . . . . 9 grams
   Dietary Fiber . . . . 2 grams
   Sugars . . . . 4 grams
Protein . . . . 4 grams
Sodium . . . . 135 milligrams

MUSHROOM CASSOULETS

6 servings/serving size: 1/2 cup

Here is a side dish that is not a bit of trouble to prepare, yet tastes delicious!

- 1 lb mushrooms, sliced
- 1 medium onion, chopped
- 1 cup low-sodium chicken broth
- 1 sprig thyme
- 1 sprig oregano
- 1 stalk of celery leaves
- 2 Tbsp lemon juice
- Fresh ground pepper
- 1/2 cup dried bread crumbs
- 2 Tbsp olive oil

1. Combine mushrooms, onion, and chicken broth in a saucepan. Tie together thyme, oregano, and celery leaves and add to mushrooms.
2. Add lemon juice and pepper, and bring to a boil. Boil until liquid is reduced, about 10 minutes.
3. Divide mushroom mixture equally into small ramekins. Mix bread crumbs and oil together, and sprinkle on top of each casserole.
4. Bake at 350 degrees for 20 minutes or until tops are golden brown. Remove from heat, and let cool slightly before serving.

....

Starch Exchange	1/2	Cholesterol	0 milligrams
Vegetable Exchange	1	Total Carbohydrate	12 grams
Fat Exchange	1	Dietary Fiber	2 grams
Calories	106	Sugars	3 grams
Total Fat	6 grams	Protein	3 grams
Saturated Fat	1 gram	Sodium	88 milligrams
Calories from Fat	50		

SAUTED SWEET PEPPERS

6 servings/serving size: 1/2 cup vegetables and about 1/3 cup rice

Add a little chicken or shrimp, and you can turn this side dish into a main meal.

- **2 medium green peppers, cut into 1-inch squares**
- **2 medium red peppers, cut into 1-inch squares**
- **1 Tbsp olive oil**
- **2 Tbsp water**
- **Fresh ground pepper**
- **1/2 tsp dried basil**
- **2 cups precooked (1 cup uncooked) rice, hot**

1. In a large skillet over medium heat, heat oil. Add peppers and saute for 3 to 5 minutes, stirring frequently.
2. Add water and pepper; continue sauteing for 4 to 5 minutes or until peppers are tender. Stir in basil and remove from heat.
3. Spread rice over a serving platter, spoon peppers and liquid on top, and serve.

....

Starch Exchange 1	Cholesterol .... 0 milligrams
Vegetable Exchange 1	Total Carbohydrate .... 20 grams
Calories 110	Dietary Fiber .... 2 grams
Total Fat .... 3 grams	Sugars .... 2 grams
Saturated Fat .... 0 grams	Protein .... 2 grams
Calories from Fat 23	Sodium .... 3 milligrams

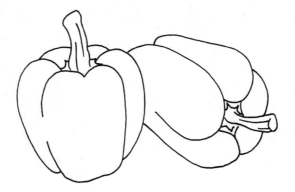

SHERRIED PEPPERS WITH BEAN SPROUTS

4 servings/serving size: 1/2 cup

*T*his side dish has so many options: add carrots, snow peas, or broccoli for more vegetables, or serve over rice or noodles or even a baked potato.

- ♦ **1 green pepper, julienned**
- ♦ **1 red pepper, julienned**
- ♦ **2 cups fresh bean sprouts**

- ♦ **2 tsp lite soy sauce**
- ♦ **1 Tbsp dry sherry**
- ♦ **1 tsp red wine vinegar**

1. In a large skillet over medium heat, combine peppers, bean sprouts, soy sauce, and sherry, mixing well. Cover and cook for 5 to 7 minutes or until vegetables are just tender.
2. Stir in vinegar and remove from heat. Serve hot.

....

Vegetable Exchange 1	Total Carbohydrate . . . . 7 grams
Calories 33	Dietary Fiber . . . . 3 grams
Total Fat . . . . 0 grams	Sugars . . . . 1 gram
Saturated Fat . . . . 0 grams	Protein . . . . 2 grams
Calories from Fat 0	Sodium . . . . 109 milligrams
Cholesterol . . . . 0 milligrams	

SNOW PEAS WITH SESAME SEEDS

6 servings/serving size: 1/2 cup

Always make sure when you cook snow peas that the cooking time is only one minute. Snow peas should be bright green and very crisp.

- ◆ **2 cups water**
- ◆ **1 lb trimmed fresh snow peas**
- ◆ **3 Tbsp sesame seeds**
- ◆ **1 Tbsp chopped shallots**
- ◆ **Fresh ground pepper**

1. Boil water in a saucepan. Add snow peas, and blanch one minute. Drain.
2. In a skillet, toast sesame seeds for 1 minute over medium heat. Add snow peas, shallots, and pepper. Continue sauteing for 1 to 2 minutes until snow peas are coated with sesame seeds. Serve.

....

Vegetable Exchange	1	Cholesterol	0 milligrams
Fat Exchange	1/2	Total Carbohydrate	6 grams
Calories	56	Dietary Fiber	2 grams
Total Fat	2 grams	Sugars	3 grams
Saturated Fat	0 grams	Protein	3 grams
Calories from Fat	22	Sodium	3 milligrams

SQUASH AND TOMATO CASSOULET

6 servings/serving size: 1/2 cup

*H*ere squash and tomatoes combine in a smooth custard sauce.

- ♦ 1 Tbsp olive oil
- ♦ 6 small yellow squash, sliced
- ♦ 1 medium onion, minced
- ♦ 2 garlic cloves, minced
- ♦ 2 Tbsp chopped parsley
- ♦ Fresh ground pepper
- ♦ 2 medium tomatoes, sliced
- ♦ 4 egg substitute equivalents
- ♦ 1 cup evaporated skim milk

1. In a large skillet over medium heat, heat oil. Add squash, onion, and garlic and saute for 5 minutes. Add parsley and pepper.
2. Layer squash mixture and tomatoes in a casserole dish. Combine eggs with evaporated milk, blending well, and pour over vegetables. Bake at 350 degrees for 20 to 25 minutes or until custard is set. Remove from oven and let cool slightly before serving.

....

Starch Exchange 1/2	Cholesterol . . . . 2 milligrams	
Vegetable Exchange 2	Total Carbohydrate . . . . 15 grams	
Fat Exchange 1/2	Dietary Fiber . . . . 2 grams	
Calories 113	Sugars . . . . 10 grams	
Total Fat . . . . 3 grams	Protein . . . . 8 grams	
Saturated Fat . . . . 0 grams	Sodium . . . . 109 milligrams	
Calories from Fat 26		

TANGY GREEN BEANS

6 servings/serving size: 1/2 cup

*P*ut some zing and zip into fresh green beans with this tasty side dish.

- 1 tsp olive oil
- 1 large onion, chopped
- 1/2 cup chopped green pepper
- 1 lb fresh green beans, trimmed

- 1 tsp dried tarragon
- 1/4 cup water
- 1 tsp lemon pepper

1. Add olive oil to a skillet, and saute onion until it is tender, about 5 or 6 minutes. Add green pepper and saute for 5 minutes more.
2. Add green beans, tarragon, water, and lemon pepper, mixing well. Cover and simmer for 10 minutes or until beans are crisp yet tender. Transfer to a bowl and serve.

....

Vegetable Exchange 2
Calories 56
Total Fat . . . . 1 gram
   Saturated Fat . . . . 0 grams
   Calories from Fat 10
Cholesterol . . . . 0 milligrams

Total Carbohydrate . . . . 11 grams
   Dietary Fiber . . . . 3 grams
   Sugars . . . . 3 grams
Protein . . . . 2 grams
Sodium . . . . 4 milligrams

VEGETABLE CONFETTI

8 servings/serving size: 1/2 cup

*E*verything but the kitchen sink is in here for a very nutritious side dish.

- 2 Tbsp olive oil
- 1/2 cup plus 2 Tbsp low-sodium chicken broth
- 1/4 cup chopped scallions
- 3 garlic cloves, minced
- 1 cup fresh broccoli, cut into florets
- 1 cup sliced zucchini
- 1 cup sliced mushrooms
- 1 cup cauliflower, broken into florets
- 3 medium potatoes, peeled and cubed
- 1 tsp dried oregano
- 1/2 tsp dried basil
- 1/2 tsp dried thyme
- 1/4 tsp paprika
- Fresh ground pepper

1. Heat olive oil and 2 Tbsp of broth in a large skillet over medium heat. Add scallions and garlic and saute for 2 minutes.
2. Add vegetables and remaining broth. Cover and simmer for 15 to 20 minutes until vegetables are cooked but crisp. Sprinkle with dried herbs and pepper and serve.

....

Vegetable Exchange 2	Cholesterol . . . . 0 milligrams
Fat Exchange 1/2	Total Carbohydrate . . . . 10 grams
Calories 78	Dietary Fiber . . . . 2 grams
Total Fat . . . . 4 grams	Sugars . . . . 2 grams
Saturated Fat . . . . 1 gram	Protein . . . . 2 grams
Calories from Fat 33	Sodium . . . . 12 milligrams

VEGETABLE-STUFFED YELLOW SQUASH

6 servings/serving size: 1 squash

Add rice into the squash shells, and top with the vegetables for a meat-free meal.

- ◆ 6 small yellow squash
- ◆ 1 tomato, finely chopped
- ◆ 1/2 cup minced onion
- ◆ 1/2 cup finely chopped green pepper
- ◆ 1/2 cup shredded low-calorie cheddar cheese
- ◆ Fresh ground pepper

1. Place squash in a large pot of boiling water. Cover, reduce heat, and simmer for 5 to 7 minutes or until squash is tender but firm. Drain and allow to cool slightly.
2. Trim stems from squash, and cut in half lengthwise. Gently scoop out the pulp, leaving a firm shell. Drain and chop the pulp.
3. In a large mixing bowl, combine pulp and the remaining ingredients, blending well.
4. Place squash shells in a 13x9x2-inch baking dish, gently spoon vegetable mixture into shells, and bake at 400 degrees for 15 to 20 minutes. Remove from oven and let cool slightly before serving.

Vegetable Exchange 2	Total Carbohydrate . . . . 8 grams
Calories 50	Dietary Fiber . . . . 2 grams
Total Fat . . . . 1 grams	Sugars . . . . 4 grams
Saturated Fat . . . . 0 grams	Protein . . . . 4 grams
Calories from Fat 10	Sodium . . . . 62 milligrams
Cholesterol . . . . 2 milligrams	

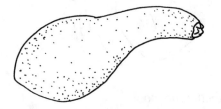

ZUCCHINI AND ONION KABOBS

8 servings/serving size: 1/2 cup

*H*ere's *a nice side dish for grilled fish, chicken, or beef.*

- ◆ **6 medium zucchini (about 4–5 oz each)**
- ◆ **4 medium red onions, quartered**
- ◆ **3/4 cup low-calorie Italian salad dressing**
- ◆ **3 Tbsp lemon juice**
- ◆ **1 large lemon, cut into wedges**

1. Combine all ingredients in a large baking dish, mixing thoroughly. Cover and let marinate, refrigerated, for 2 to 3 hours. Remove vegetables from marinade (reserving marinade), and alternate zucchini and onion on skewers.
2. Grill kabobs 6 inches above medium heat, basting frequently, for about 20 minutes. Transfer to a platter, and garnish with lemon wedges. Serve with remaining marinade.

....

Vegetable Exchange 2	Total Carbohydrate . . . . 13 grams
Calories 61	Dietary Fiber . . . . 2 grams
Total Fat . . . . 1 gram	Sugars . . . . 9 grams
Saturated Fat . . . . 0 grams	Protein . . . . 2 grams
Calories from Fat 7	Sodium . . . . 324 milligrams
Cholesterol . . . . 0 milligrams	

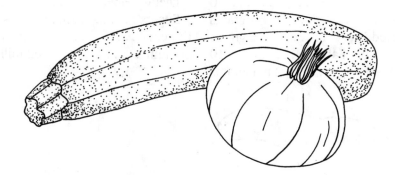

ZUCCHINI SAUTE

4 servings/serving size: 1/2 cup

*R*ed *onion gives this zucchini a sweetness that is irresistible.*

- ◆ **1 Tbsp olive oil**
- ◆ **1 medium red onion, chopped**
- ◆ **3 medium zucchini (about 5 to 6 oz each), cut into rounds**

- ◆ **1/4 tsp dried oregano**
- ◆ **Fresh ground pepper**

1. In a large skillet over medium heat, heat oil. Add onion, and saute until onion is translucent but not browned.
2. Add zucchini, cover, and simmer 3 to 4 minutes. Sprinkle with oregano and pepper, and serve hot.

Vegetable Exchange 1
Fat Exchange 1
Calories 62
Total Fat . . . . 3 grams
   Saturated Fat . . . . 0 grams
   Calories from Fat 31
Cholesterol . . . . 0 milligrams
Total Carbohydrate . . . . 8 grams
   Dietary Fiber . . . . 2 grams
   Sugars . . . . 5 grams
Protein . . . . 1 gram
Sodium . . . . 4 milligrams

RICE & POTATOES

ASIAN FRIED RICE

4 servings/serving size: 1/2 cup

*N*ow you can make this traditional favorite at home!

- 2 Tbsp peanut oil
- 1/4 cup chopped onion
- 1/2 cup sliced carrot
- 2 Tbsp chopped green pepper
- 2 cups cooked rice
- 1/2 cup water chestnuts, drained
- 1/2 cup sliced mushrooms
- 2 Tbsp lite soy sauce
- 3 egg substitute equivalents, beaten
- 1/2 cup sliced scallions

1. In a large skillet, heat oil. Saute onion, carrot, and green pepper for 5 to 6 minutes.
2. Stir in rice, water chestnuts, mushrooms, and soy sauce, and continue to cook for 8 to 10 minutes.
3. Stir in eggs, and continue to cook for another 3 minutes. Top with sliced scallions to serve.

....

Starch Exchange	2	Cholesterol	0 milligrams
Fat Exchange	1	Total Carbohydrate	31 grams
Calories	217	Dietary Fiber	2 grams
Total Fat	7 grams	Sugars	4 grams
Saturated Fat	1 gram	Protein	7 grams
Calories from Fat	66	Sodium	377 milligrams

BAKED POTATO TOPPERS

Try these ideas to spice up your spud! Start by baking an 8-oz potato for about 50–60 minutes in a 350-degree oven.

◆ Create a pizza potato: Add 2 Tbsp of your favorite tomato sauce and 1 Tbsp of grated Parmesan cheese. Place potato in oven to melt cheese.

Starch Exchange 3	Total Carbohydrate . . . . 49 grams
Calories 233	Dietary Fiber . . . . 5 grams
Total Fat . . . . 2 grams	Sugars . . . . 4 grams
Saturated Fat . . . . 1 gram	Protein . . . . 7 grams
Calories from Fat 16	Sodium . . . . 285 milligrams
Cholesterol . . . . 4 milligrams	

◆ Spruce up 1 Tbsp low-fat sour cream with 1 tsp chopped chives, thyme, rosemary, or scallions.

Starch Exchange 3	Total Carbohydrate . . . . 48 grams
Calories 222	Dietary Fiber . . . . 4 grams
Total Fat . . . . 1 gram	Sugars . . . . 5 grams
Saturated Fat . . . . 1 gram	Protein . . . . 5 grams
Calories from Fat 11	Sodium . . . . 35 milligrams
Cholesterol . . . . 0 milligrams	

◆ For more of a main meal, top potatoes with 1/4 cup chopped cooked chicken mixed with 2 Tbsp salsa.

Starch Exchange 3	Cholesterol . . . . 36 milligrams
Lean Meat Exchange 1	Total Carbohydrate . . . . 48 grams
Calories 278	Dietary Fiber . . . . 5 grams
Total Fat . . . . 2 grams	Sugars . . . . 4 grams
Saturated Fat . . . . 0 grams	Protein . . . . 18 grams
Calories from Fat 16	Sodium . . . . 127 milligrams

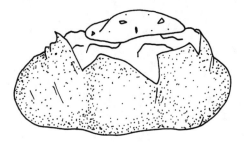

COLORFUL RICE CASSEROLE

12 servings/serving size: 1/4 cup rice plus 1/2 cup vegetables

Use this recipe when zucchini are at their best.

- 1 Tbsp olive oil
- 1-1/2 lb zucchini, thinly sliced
- 3/4 cup chopped scallions
- 2 cups corn kernels (frozen or fresh; if frozen, defrost)
- 16-oz can no-salt-added chopped tomatoes, undrained

- 1/4 cup chopped parsley
- 1 tsp oregano
- 3 cups cooked rice (white or brown)

1. In a large skillet, heat oil. Add zucchini and scallions, and saute for 5 minutes.
2. Add remaining ingredients, cover, reduce heat, and simmer for 10 to 15 minutes or until vegetables are heated through. Transfer to a bowl and serve.

....

Starch Exchange 1	Cholesterol . . . . 0 milligrams
Vegetable Exchange 1	Total Carbohydrate . . . . 23 grams
Calories 108	Dietary Fiber . . . . 3 grams
Total Fat . . . . 1 gram	Sugars . . . . 5 grams
Saturated Fat . . . . 0 grams	Protein . . . . 3 grams
Calories from Fat 12	Sodium . . . . 106 milligrams

CURRIED RICE WITH PINEAPPLE

4 servings/serving size: about 1/2 cup

*S*weet pineapple sparks the flavor in this side dish.

- ◆ 1 onion, chopped
- ◆ 1-1/2 cups water
- ◆ 1-1/4 cups low-sodium beef broth
- ◆ 1 cup uncooked rice
- ◆ 1 tsp curry powder
- ◆ 1/4 tsp garlic powder
- ◆ 8 oz pineapple chunks, drained

1. In a medium saucepan, combine onion, water, and beef broth. Bring to a boil, and add rice, curry powder, and garlic powder. Cover and reduce heat. Simmer for 25 minutes.
2. Add pineapple and continue to simmer 5 to 7 minutes more until rice is tender and water is absorbed. Transfer to a serving bowl and serve.

Starch Exchange 3
Calories 215
Total Fat .... 1 gram
  Saturated Fat .... 0 grams
  Calories from Fat 8
Cholesterol .... 0 milligrams
Total Carbohydrate .... 46 grams
  Dietary Fiber .... 2 grams
  Sugars .... 7 grams
Protein .... 5 grams
Sodium .... 21 milligrams

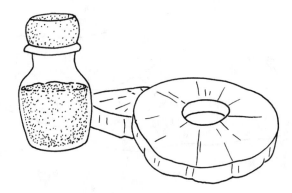

FESTIVE SWEET POTATOES

8 servings/serving size: 1/2 cup

*F*orget gobs of brown sugar and butter. Pineapple and spices add flavor, not fat.

- **4 sweet potatoes (about 20 oz total)**
- **2 cups crushed pineapple, in its own juice**
- **2 tsp cinnamon**
- **1 tsp nutmeg**
- **1 Tbsp slivered almonds**

1. In a large saucepan, boil potatoes over medium heat for about 45 minutes until you can pierce them easily with a fork (or bake them directly on a rack in a preheated 350-degree oven for 45 minutes).
2. Let potatoes cool, and then gently peel them.
3. Mash potatoes with pineapple and spices and place in a casserole dish coated with nonstick cooking spray. Top casserole with almonds and bake for 20 minutes at 350 degrees.

....

Starch Exchange 1	Total Carbohydrate . . . . 19 grams
Calories 84	Dietary Fiber . . . . 2 grams
Total Fat . . . . 1 gram	Sugars . . . . 11 grams
Saturated Fat . . . . 0 grams	Protein . . . . 1 gram
Calories from Fat 5	Sodium . . . . 7 milligrams
Cholesterol . . . . 0 milligrams	

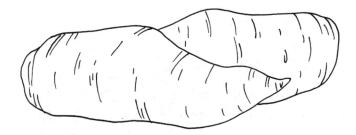

POTATO PARMESAN CHIPS

8 servings/serving size: 1/2 potato

These tasty and colorful chips are a change from the usual plain potato.

- ◆ **4 large potatoes (4 to 5 oz each)**
- ◆ **2 Tbsp olive oil**
- ◆ **1 tsp grated onion**
- ◆ **Dash salt**
- ◆ **Fresh ground pepper**
- ◆ **1/4 tsp paprika**
- ◆ **2 Tbsp grated Parmesan cheese**

1. Wash and cut unpeeled potatoes into 1/8-inch thick slices. Place in a single layer over baking sheets coated with cooking spray.
2. Heat oil in a small skillet and add onion, salt, pepper, and paprika. Brush potatoes with oil mixture and bake at 425 degrees for 15 to 20 minutes or until potatoes are crispy and golden brown.
3. Remove from oven and sprinkle with cheese. Serve.

....

Starch Exchange 1	Cholesterol . . . . 1 milligram
Fat Exchange 1/2	Total Carbohydrate . . . . 16 grams
Calories 105	Dietary Fiber . . . . 2 grams
Total Fat . . . . 4 grams	Sugars . . . . 1 gram
Saturated Fat . . . . 1 gram	Protein . . . . 2 grams
Calories from Fat 34	Sodium . . . . 46 milligrams

RICE PARMESAN

4 servings/serving size: about 1/2 cup

Y*ou can probably make this dish anytime with ingredients you have on hand.*

- 1 Tbsp olive oil
- 1 medium onion, chopped
- 1 garlic clove, minced
- 1 cup low-sodium chicken broth

- 1 cup uncooked rice
- 1/2 cup dry white wine
- 1/2 cup grated Parmesan cheese

1. In a skillet over medium heat, heat oil. Add onion and garlic and saute for 8 minutes.
2. Stir in chicken broth, rice, and wine and bring to a boil. Reduce heat to low, cover, and continue cooking for 20 to 25 minutes or until liquid is absorbed. Transfer to a serving bowl, and add cheese before serving.

Starch Exchange	3	Cholesterol	8 milligrams
Fat Exchange	1	Total Carbohydrate	42 grams
Calories	279	Dietary Fiber	1 gram
Total Fat	7 grams	Sugars	4 grams
Saturated Fat	3 grams	Protein	9 grams
Calories from Fat	64	Sodium	204 milligrams

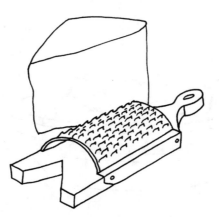

RICE WITH SPINACH AND FETA

6 servings/serving size: 1/3 cup

Here's rice with a Greek twist.

- 1 cup uncooked rice
- 1 cup low-sodium chicken broth
- 1 cup water
- 1 Tbsp olive oil
- 1 medium onion, chopped
- 1 cup sliced mushrooms
- 2 garlic cloves, minced
- 1 Tbsp lemon juice
- 1/2 tsp dried oregano
- 6 cups fresh spinach, stems trimmed, washed, patted dry, and coarsely chopped
- 4 oz feta cheese, crumbled
- Fresh ground pepper

1. In a medium saucepan over medium heat, combine rice, chicken broth, and water. Bring to a boil, cover, reduce heat, and simmer for 15 minutes. Transfer to a serving bowl.
2. In a skillet, heat oil. Saute onion, mushrooms, and garlic for 5 to 7 minutes. Stir in lemon juice and oregano. Add spinach, cheese, and pepper, tossing until spinach is slightly wilted. Toss with rice and serve.

....

Starch Exchange	2	
Fat Exchange	1	
Calories	219	
Total Fat	7 grams	
Saturated Fat	3 grams	
Calories from Fat	64	

Cholesterol	17 milligrams
Total Carbohydrate	32 grams
Dietary Fiber	3 grams
Sugars	3 grams
Protein	8 grams
Sodium	265 milligrams

SAGE POTATOES

4 servings/serving size: 1/2 potato

*T*his dish is a good addition to your brunch table.

- ◆ **2 Tbsp olive oil**
- ◆ **1 small onion, chopped**
- ◆ **1 garlic clove, minced**
- ◆ **1 tsp dried sage**

- ◆ **2 potatoes (4 to 5 oz each), unpeeled, halved lengthwise, and sliced crosswise into thin slices**

1. In a large skillet over medium heat, heat oil. Add onion and garlic and saute for 2 to 3 minutes.
2. Add sage and potatoes, cover, and cook for 10 minutes, stirring occasionally. Turn potatoes over with a spatula, and continue to cook for another 5 to 7 minutes until golden brown. Serve.

....

Starch Exchange 1	Cholesterol . . . . 0 milligrams
Fat Exchange 1-1/2	Total Carbohydrate . . . . 19 grams
Calories 142	Dietary Fiber . . . . 2 grams
Total Fat . . . . 7 grams	Sugars . . . . 3 grams
Saturated Fat . . . . 1 gram	Protein . . . . 2 grams
Calories from Fat 62	Sodium . . . . 6 milligrams

SCALLOPED POTATOES

8 servings/serving size: 1/2 cup

These potatoes are still creamy and rich, but with far less fat.

- **6 medium potatoes (4 oz each), unpeeled**
- **4 cups water**
- **1 Tbsp olive oil**
- **1/3 cup chopped onion**
- **2 egg substitute equivalents**
- **1 cup low-fat sour cream**
- **Fresh ground pepper**
- **2 oz low-fat cheddar cheese, shredded**

1. Wash potatoes and place in a saucepan with water. Bring to a boil, lower the heat, and let potatoes cook for 25 minutes. Drain potatoes, let cool, and slice into 1/4-inch slices.
2. Heat oil in a skillet. Add onion and saute for 5 minutes. Add onion to egg, sour cream, and pepper in a bowl and mix well.
3. Lay potato slices in a casserole dish. Spoon sour cream mixture over potatoes. Top with cheese.
4. Bake for 35 minutes at 350 degrees until top is browned.

....

Starch Exchange 1-1/2
Fat Exchange 1/2
Calories 149
Total Fat . . . . 4 grams
   Saturated Fat . . . . 2 grams
   Calories from Fat 39

Cholesterol . . . . 2 milligrams
Total Carbohydrate . . . . 22 grams
   Dietary Fiber . . . . 2 grams
   Sugars . . . . 6 grams
Protein . . . . 7 grams
Sodium . . . . 108 milligrams

BREADS & MUFFINS

BANANA CARROT MUFFINS

12 servings/serving size: 1 muffin

These muffins are moist, sweet, and full of good-for-you ingredients!

- 1-1/2 cups whole-wheat or unbleached flour
- 2 tsp baking powder
- 1 tsp baking soda
- 1/2 tsp nutmeg
- Pinch cloves
- 2 egg substitute equivalents
- 1/2 cup unsweetened applesauce
- 2 Tbsp fructose
- 1/2 cup low-fat buttermilk
- 1/2 cup mashed banana
- 1 cup grated carrot
- 1 tsp vanilla

1. Preheat the oven to 400 degrees. Combine the first 5 ingredients in a large bowl. Combine the remaining ingredients in a smaller bowl. Combine all ingredients together and mix well, but do not overbeat.
2. Spoon into muffin cups and bake for 20 minutes. Serve warm or at room temperature.

....

Starch Exchange 1
Calories 88
Total Fat .... 0 grams
   Saturated Fat .... 0 grams
   Calories from Fat 3
Cholesterol .... 0 milligrams
Total Carbohydrate .... 18 grams
   Dietary Fiber .... 1 gram
   Sugars .... 5 grams
Protein .... 3 grams
Sodium .... 149 milligrams

BUTTERMILK BISCUITS

12 servings/serving size: 1 biscuit

These biscuits are great with thick, chunky stews.

- 2 cups whole-wheat pastry flour or unbleached white flour
- 1 Tbsp baking powder
- 1/2 tsp baking soda
- 1 cup low-fat buttermilk
- 3 Tbsp canola oil

1. Preheat the oven to 425 degrees. Lightly spray two cookie sheets with nonstick cooking spray.
2. In a medium bowl, combine the flour, baking powder, and baking soda. Add the buttermilk and oil; mix with a fork until well blended.
3. Drop the dough by heaping tablespoonfuls onto cookie sheets, 1-1/2 inches apart. Bake for 10 to 12 minutes until lightly browned.

....

Starch Exchange 1	Cholesterol .... 1 milligram
Fat Exchange 1/2	Total Carbohydrate .... 17 grams
Calories 116	Dietary Fiber .... 1 gram
Total Fat .... 4 grams	Sugars .... 1 gram
Saturated Fat .... 0 grams	Protein .... 3 grams
Calories from Fat 35	Sodium .... 134 milligrams

CORN MUFFINS

12 servings/serving size: 1 muffin

Use some of the variations included below to create interesting corn muffins. (The variations do not significantly alter the nutrient exchange information.)

- ◆ **1 cup yellow cornmeal**
- ◆ **1/2 tsp baking soda**
- ◆ **1/2 tsp baking powder**
- ◆ **1/4 tsp salt (optional)**

- ◆ **1 cup low-fat buttermilk**
- ◆ **1 egg substitute equivalent**
- ◆ **1 Tbsp canola oil**

1. Preheat the oven to 425 degrees. Combine the cornmeal, baking soda, baking powder, and salt; mix thoroughly. Stir in buttermilk, egg, and oil; blend well.
2. Coat muffin pans with nonstick cooking spray. Spoon batter into muffin pans, filling the cups 2/3 full. Bake for 10 to 12 minutes or until tops are golden brown. Serve warm.

Variations: add 1/2 cup cooked corn kernels, 1/2 cup finely diced green or red pepper, or 1/2 cup finely diced sauted onions to the batter.

....

Starch Exchange 1	Total Carbohydrate .... 10 grams
Calories 164	Dietary Fiber .... 1 gram
Total Fat .... 2 grams	Sugars .... 1 gram
Saturated Fat .... 0 grams	Protein .... 2 grams
Calories from Fat 14	Sodium .... 120 milligrams
Cholesterol .... 1 milligram	w/o added salt ...... 76 milligrams

CRANBERRY ORANGE SCONES

8 servings/serving size: 1 scone

These scones—low in fat and homemade—are wonderful with soup or salad.

- 1/2 cup dried cranberries
- 2 Tbsp fructose
- 1/2 cup low-fat buttermilk, room temperature
- 3/4 cup fresh orange juice
- Grated peel of 1 large orange
- 2-1/4 cups whole-wheat pastry flour or unbleached flour
- 1 tsp baking soda
- 1 tsp cream of tartar
- 1/2 tsp salt
- 2 Tbsp low-calorie margarine, cold

1. Preheat the oven to 375 degrees. Sprinkle a cookie sheet with flour. Soak the dried cranberries in boiling water for 5 minutes. Drain and set aside. In a small bowl, mix together the fructose and buttermilk. Add orange juice and rind.
2. Sift flour, baking soda, cream of tartar, and salt in a large bowl. Using a fork or fingers, cut in the margarine until well combined. Stir the buttermilk mixture and cranberries into flour mixture and mix very gently by hand until combined.
3. Turn out the batter onto the floured cookie sheet and pat into a circle about 3/4 inch thick, 8 inches across. Using a sharp knife, cut the circle into 8 wedges.
4. Place the pan in the oven and bake for 25 minutes. Cool and cut completely through the wedge cuts to serve.

....

Starch Exchange	2-1/2	Total Carbohydrate	40 grams
Calories	195	Dietary Fiber	1 gram
Total Fat	2 grams	Sugars	13 grams
Saturated Fat	0 grams	Protein	5 grams
Calories from Fat	18	Sodium	275 milligrams
Cholesterol	1 milligram		

DATE NUT BREAD

16 servings/serving size: one 1-inch slice

This bread tastes great with fruit or chicken salads.

- 1-3/4 cups chopped, pitted dates
- 1-1/4 cups boiling water
- 2-1/4 cups whole-wheat flour
- 1/2 cup chopped walnuts
- 1 tsp baking soda
- 1 egg substitute equivalent
- 1/2 cup unsweetened applesauce
- 2 Tbsp fructose
- 1 tsp vanilla or almond extract

1. In a bowl, combine the dates and boiling water; let stand for 15 minutes. Lightly coat a 9x5-inch loaf pan with nonstick cooking spray. Preheat the oven to 350 degrees.
2. In a large bowl, combine the flour, nuts, and baking soda. Add the egg, applesauce, fructose, and extract. Add the dates and mix well.
3. Pour mixture into the prepared pan and bake for 65 minutes or until a toothpick inserted in the center comes out clean. Cool in the pan on a rack for 10 minutes. Remove from the pan and serve warm or cold.

....

Starch Exchange	1	Cholesterol	0 milligrams
Fruit Exchange	1	Total Carbohydrate	28 grams
Calories	140	Dietary Fiber	4 grams
Total Fat	3 grams	Sugars	14 grams
Saturated Fat	0 grams	Protein	3 grams
Calories from Fat	23	Sodium	58 milligrams

HOMEMADE SEASONED BREAD CRUMBS

8 servings/serving size: 1/4 cup

These homemade seasoned bread crumbs are much lower in sodium than the store-bought variety, and are very easy to make!

- 1/3 loaf low-calorie store-bought bread
- 2 tsp garlic powder
- 1 tsp dried basil
- 1 tsp dried oregano
- 1 tsp onion powder
- 1/4 tsp paprika
- 1/4 tsp salt
- 1/4 tsp pepper

Leave the bread out on the kitchen counter to dry for 2 days. Remove the crusts and tear the bread into bite-sized pieces. Place the bread in the food processor or blender along with the spices and blend to make crumbs.

....

Starch Exchange 1/2	Total Carbohydrate .... 9 grams
Calories 42	Dietary Fiber .... 2 grams
Total Fat .... 1 gram	Sugars .... 1 gram
Saturated Fat .... 0 grams	Protein .... 2 grams
Calories from Fat 5	Sodium .... 158 milligrams
Cholesterol .... 0 milligrams	

IRISH SODA BREAD

10 servings/serving size: one 1-inch slice

There is nothing like warm Irish soda bread!

- ◆ **2 cups unbleached white flour**
- ◆ **1 tsp baking soda**
- ◆ **2 Tbsp low-calorie margarine, chilled and cut into bits**
- ◆ **1 Tbsp caraway seeds**
- ◆ **1/4 cup dried currants or raisins**
- ◆ **1 cup low-fat buttermilk**

1. Preheat the oven to 375 degrees. Combine the flour and baking soda. With 2 knives or a pastry blender, work in the margarine until the mixture resembles coarse crumbs.

2. Toss in the caraway seeds and currants. With a fork, mix in the buttermilk and mix until just blended. Turn the dough out onto a lightly floured surface and knead very gently for 20 strokes, just until smooth. Do not overwork the dough.

3. Pat well into a 9-inch pan or shape well on a baking sheet. Make a shallow 4-inch cross in the center of the loaf and bake for 25 to 30 minutes until golden. Serve warm.

....

Starch Exchange	1-1/2	Total Carbohydrate	23 grams
Calories	122	Dietary Fiber	1 gram
Total Fat	2 grams	Sugars	4 grams
Saturated Fat	0 grams	Protein	4 grams
Calories from Fat	14	Sodium	127 milligrams
Cholesterol	1 milligram		

PINEAPPLE MUFFINS

12 servings/serving size: 1 muffin

These are a welcome addition to the breakfast table. Just add fruit or juice and yogurt.

- 1-1/2 cups whole-wheat or pastry flour
- 2 tsp baking powder
- 1/2 tsp baking soda
- 1/4 cup fructose
- 2 tsp cinnamon
- 2 egg substitute equivalents
- 2/3 cup unsweetened applesauce
- 1 cup crushed canned pineapple, drained
- 1/2 cup diced dried apricots

1. In a medium bowl, combine dry ingredients.
2. In a large bowl, combine remaining ingredients. Slowly add dry ingredients to wet ingredients and mix until blended. Do not beat.
3. Place batter into prepared muffin cups, filling 2/3 full.
4. Bake at 350 degrees for 25 minutes until golden brown.

....

Starch Exchange 1	Cholesterol . . . . 0 milligrams
Fruit Exchange 1/2	Total Carbohydrate . . . . 21 grams
Calories 95	Dietary Fiber . . . . 3 grams
Total Fat . . . . 0 grams	Sugars . . . . 9 grams
Saturated Fat . . . . 0 grams	Protein . . . . 3 grams
Calories from Fat 0	Sodium . . . . 101 milligrams

SPOON BREAD

16 servings/serving size: 1/2 cup

Old-fashioned spoon bread is great with any meal!

- 2 cups water
- 2 cups yellow cornmeal
- 2 tsp baking powder
- 1 tsp salt (optional)

- 1-1/2 tsp baking soda
- 2 cups skim milk
- 2 egg substitute equivalents

1. In a bowl, combine 1 cup of the water with the cornmeal, baking powder, salt, and baking soda.
2. In a 3-quart saucepan, heat the remaining 1 cup water to boiling; reduce the heat to low and stir in the cornmeal mixture. Cook the mixture until thick and remove from heat.
3. Preheat the oven to 350 degrees. Lightly spray a 2-quart casserole dish with nonstick cooking spray. First add the milk, then the eggs, into the cornmeal mixture and beat until smooth. Pour into the casserole dish. Bake for 1 hour until set; serve warm.

....

Starch Exchange	1	Total Carbohydrate	15 grams
Calories	79	Dietary Fiber	1 gram
Total Fat	0 grams	Sugars	1 gram
Saturated Fat	0 grams	Protein	3 grams
Calories from Fat	3	Sodium	276 milligrams
Cholesterol	1 milligram	w/o added salt	142 milligrams

SWEET POTATO AND ZUCCHINI BREAD

16 servings/serving size: one 1-inch slice

This fiber-rich, slightly spicy bread is especially good around holiday time.

- 2 cups whole-wheat or unbleached flour
- 1 tsp baking powder
- 1/2 tsp baking soda
- 2 tsp cinnamon
- 3 egg substitute equivalents
- 3/4 cup unsweetened applesauce
- 1/4 cup fructose
- 1 tsp vanilla extract
- 1-1/2 cups grated zucchini, unpeeled
- 1-1/2 cups grated raw sweet potato, peeled

1. Preheat the oven to 350 degrees. Spray a 9x5x3-inch loaf pan with nonstick cooking spray and set aside.
2. Combine the first four ingredients in a medium bowl. In a larger bowl, beat together the eggs, applesauce, fructose, and vanilla. Mix in the zucchini and sweet potatoes. Add the flour mixture to the bowl and mix well.
3. Transfer the batter to the prepared pan; bake for 1 hour and 15 minutes. Cool bread in the pan for 15 minutes. Turn bread onto a rack and cool completely. Slice and serve.

....

Starch Exchange 1	Total Carbohydrate . . . . 19 grams
Calories 89	Dietary Fiber . . . . 1 gram
Total Fat . . . . 0 grams	Sugars . . . . 6 grams
Saturated Fat . . . . 0 grams	Protein . . . . 3 grams
Calories from Fat 2	Sodium . . . . 68 milligrams
Cholesterol . . . . 0 milligrams	

BREAKFASTS

BAKED FRENCH TOAST WITH RASPBERRY SAUCE

4 servings/serving size: 2 slices

Here is French toast that you soak overnight in a tasty batter and let puff up in the oven.

- ◆ **4 egg substitute equivalents**
- ◆ **2/3 cup skim milk**
- ◆ **1 tsp maple extract**
- ◆ **1 tsp cinnamon**
- ◆ **1/2 tsp nutmeg**
- ◆ **8 slices whole-wheat bread**

- ◆ **2 cups frozen or fresh raspberries**
- ◆ **1 Tbsp orange juice**
- ◆ **1 tsp vanilla extract**
- ◆ **2 tsp cornstarch**

1. Beat together eggs, milk, maple extract, cinnamon, and nutmeg in a medium bowl.
2. In a casserole dish, lay bread slices side by side. Pour over the egg-milk mixture, cover, and place in refrigerator overnight.
3. The next day, bake the French toast at 350 degrees for about 30 minutes until golden brown and slightly puffed.
4. To make raspberry sauce, puree raspberries in a blender. Strain to remove seeds. In a small saucepan, combine pureed berries with orange juice, vanilla, and cornstarch. Bring to a boil and cook for 1 minute until mixture is thickened. Serve over French toast.

....

Starch Exchange 2-1/2	Total Carbohydrate . . . . 38 grams
Calories 216	Dietary Fiber . . . . 8 grams
Total Fat . . . . 3 grams	Sugars . . . . 8 grams
Saturated Fat . . . . 1 gram	Protein . . . . 12 grams
Calories from Fat 25	Sodium . . . . 400 milligrams
Cholesterol . . . . 1 milligram	

BLUEBERRY SCONES

8 servings/serving size: 1 3-inch scone

Typical store-bought scones have a lot more fat and calories than these.

- 1/2 cup buttermilk at room temperature
- 3/4 cup orange juice
- Grated peel of 1 orange
- 2-1/4 cups whole-wheat pastry flour or unbleached white flour
- 1 tsp baking soda
- 1 tsp cream of tartar
- 3 Tbsp fructose
- 2 Tbsp low-calorie margarine, cold
- 1 cup fresh or frozen (thawed) blueberries

1. In a small bowl, combine buttermilk, orange juice, and orange peel. Set aside.
2. Sift together flour, baking soda, cream of tartar, and fructose into a large bowl. Using a fork or pastry blender, cut in the margarine until well combined. Stir in buttermilk mixture and blueberries, and mix gently by hand until well combined.
3. Turn batter onto a lightly floured cookie sheet, and pat into a circle about 3/4 inch thick and 8 inches across. Use a sharp knife to cut the circle into eight wedges, cutting almost all the way through. Place pan in a preheated 375-degree oven, and bake for 25 minutes until lightly browned.

....

Starch Exchange	2	Total Carbohydrate	33 grams
Calories	168	Dietary Fiber	5 grams
Total Fat	2 grams	Sugars	9 grams
Saturated Fat	0 grams	Protein	5 grams
Calories from Fat	20	Sodium	144 milligrams
Cholesterol	1 milligram		

CORN CAKES

6 servings/serving size: 2 4-inch cakes

These are not only good for breakfast, but for a light dinner, too.

- **2/3 cup unbleached white flour**
- **1/3 cup whole-wheat or pastry flour**
- **2 tsp baking powder**
- **1 Tbsp fructose**
- **3/4 cup buttermilk**
- **1 egg substitute equivalent**
- **2 Tbsp canola oil**
- **1 cup corn kernels (frozen or fresh; if frozen, defrost)**

1. Combine all dry ingredients in a medium bowl.
2. In another bowl, combine buttermilk, egg, and oil. Stir in corn kernels. Slowly add this mixture to dry ingredients, just to blend. A few lumps will remain.
3. On a heated nonstick griddle, pour 1/4 cup batter per cake. Cook cakes for about 3 minutes, flip them over, and cook 1 to 2 minutes more, until golden brown. Serve.

....

Starch Exchange	1-1/2	Cholesterol	1 milligram
Fat Exchange	1	Total Carbohydrate	24 grams
Calories	161	Dietary Fiber	2 grams
Total Fat	5 grams	Sugars	4 grams
Saturated Fat	1 gram	Protein	5 grams
Calories from Fat	47	Sodium	151 milligrams

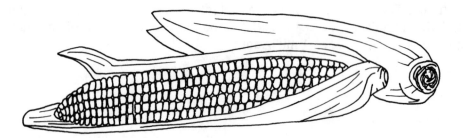

FRESH BLUEBERRY PANCAKES

8 servings/serving size: 2 4- to 5-inch pancakes

*W*hat's breakfast without a stack of warm blueberry pancakes?

- 1 cup flour
- 1/2 tsp baking soda
- 1-1/2 tsp baking powder
- 1 egg substitute equivalent

- 1 cup low-fat buttermilk
- 1 Tbsp canola oil
- 1/2 cup fresh blueberries, washed and drained

1. Combine dry ingredients in a medium-sized bowl and set aside.
2. In a small bowl, combine egg, buttermilk, and oil and mix well. Add mixture to the dry ingredients, stirring until moistened, then gently fold in the blueberries.
3. Coat a griddle or skillet with cooking spray. Pour 2 Tbsp of batter for each pancake onto hot griddle. Turn the pancakes when tops are covered with tiny bubbles and edges are golden brown.

Starch Exchange 1
Fat Exchange 1/2
Calories 94
Total Fat . . . . 2 grams
   Saturated Fat . . . . 0 grams
   Calories from Fat 20
Cholesterol . . . . 1 milligram
Total Carbohydrate . . . . 15 grams
   Dietary Fiber . . . . 1 gram
   Sugars . . . . 3 grams
Protein . . . . 3 grams
Sodium . . . . 153 milligrams

FRUIT PUFF PANCAKE

4 servings/serving size: 1/4 recipe

*T*his recipe is elegant to serve at brunch.

- **5 egg substitute equivalents**
- **1/2 cup skim milk**
- **1/2 cup flour**
- **1 Tbsp vanilla extract**

- **4 cups mixed fresh fruit** (try sliced strawberries, blueberries, and bananas)

1. Preheat the oven to 425 degrees. Spray a pie plate or oven-proof skillet with nonstick cooking spray. In a large bowl, combine the eggs and milk. Add the flour and vanilla.
2. Pour the batter into the prepared pan and place it in the oven. Bake for 15 to 20 minutes until batter is puffed and edges are browned. Remove the puff pancake, fill the center with the fruit, cut into wedges, and serve.

Starch Exchange 1-1/2
Fruit Exchange 1
Calories 184
Total Fat . . . . 1 gram
  Saturated Fat . . . . 0 grams
  Calories from Fat 7
Cholesterol . . . . 1 milligram
Total Carbohydrate . . . . 36 grams
  Dietary Fiber . . . . 4 grams
  Sugars . . . . 16 grams
Protein . . . . 10 grams
Sodium . . . . 120 milligrams

HASH BROWNS

4 servings/serving size: 1/2 cup

*L*ove *hash browns, but not the fat content? Don't worry with these greaseless, yet tasty, potatoes.*

- **2 large baking potatoes (about 10 oz each)**
- **2 Tbsp minced onion**
- **1 tsp garlic powder**
- **1/2 tsp dried thyme**
- **Fresh ground pepper**

1. Peel and shred each potato with a hand grater or a food processor with grater attachment. Combine potatoes with onion and spices.
2. Coat a large skillet with cooking spray and place over medium heat until hot.
3. Pack potato mixture firmly into skillet; cook mixture for 6–8 minutes or until bottom is browned. Invert potato patty onto a plate and return to the skillet, cooked side up.
4. Continue cooking over medium heat for another 6–8 minutes until bottom is browned. Remove from heat and cut into 4 wedges.

....

Starch Exchange	1-1/2	Total Carbohydrate	23 grams
Calories	100	Dietary Fiber	2 grams
Total Fat	0 grams	Sugars	2 grams
Saturated Fat	0 grams	Protein	2 grams
Calories from Fat	0	Sodium	2 milligrams
Cholesterol	0 milligrams		

ITALIAN FRITTATA

4 servings/serving size: 1/4 recipe

You can serve this open-faced egg dish for casual breakfasts, too.

- 1/2 tsp olive oil
- 5 egg substitute equivalents
- 2 cups mixed steamed vegetables (try chopped broccoli, asparagus, and red peppers)
- 2 tsp minced garlic
- 2 Tbsp minced chives
- 1 tsp dried oregano
- 1 tsp dried basil
- Fresh ground pepper
- 1/4 cup fresh grated Parmesan cheese

1. Add the oil to an ovenproof skillet or pie plate. In a large bowl, combine the remaining ingredients and add to the skillet.
2. Set the skillet in the oven and bake the frittata for 14 to 17 minutes until set. Remove from the oven and loosen edges with a spatula. Sprinkle with grated cheese, cut into wedges, and serve.

....

Vegetable Exchange 1	Cholesterol . . . . 4 milligrams
Lean Meat Exchange 1	Total Carbohydrate . . . . 6 grams
Calories 82	Dietary Fiber . . . . 3 grams
Total Fat . . . . 2 grams	Sugars . . . . 3 grams
Saturated Fat . . . . 1 gram	Protein . . . . 10 grams
Calories from Fat 20	Sodium . . . . 203 milligrams

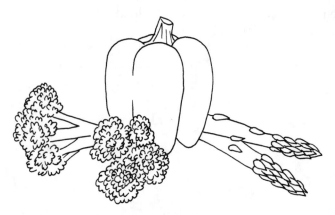

MINI BREAKFAST QUICHES

12 servings/serving size: 1 muffin cup

You can also serve these mini quiches as an appetizer.

- **4 oz diced green chilies**
- **2 oz diced pimentos, drained**
- **3 cups precooked white rice**
- **2 egg substitute equivalents**
- **1/3 cup skim milk**
- **1/2 tsp cumin**
- **Dash salt and pepper**
- **1 cup low-fat cheddar cheese**

1. Preheat the oven to 400 degrees. In a large mixing bowl, combine all ingredients except 1/2 cup of the cheese.
2. Spoon mixture evenly into muffin cups and sprinkle with remaining cheese. Bake for 12 to 15 minutes or until set. Carefully remove the quiches from the pan, arrange on a platter, and serve.

....

Starch Exchange 1
Calories 88
Total Fat . . . . 2 grams
   Saturated Fat . . . . 1 gram
   Calories from Fat 16
Cholesterol . . . . 7 milligrams

Total Carbohydrate . . . . 13 grams
   Dietary Fiber . . . . 0 grams
   Sugars . . . . 1 gram
Protein . . . . 5 grams
Sodium . . . . 98 milligrams

TURKEY SAUSAGE PATTIES

4 servings/serving size: about 2 oz

*P*repare these one day in advance, and the flavor will be even better.

- ◆ **1/2 lb ground turkey**
- ◆ **1/4 cup low-sodium beef broth**
- ◆ **1/2 Tbsp lemon juice**
- ◆ **2 Tbsp fine dried bread crumbs**
- ◆ **1/8 tsp fennel seeds**
- ◆ **1/8 tsp ground ginger**
- ◆ **1/2 tsp grated lemon peel**
- ◆ **1/4 tsp fresh minced sage**
- ◆ **Fresh ground pepper**
- ◆ **1/8 tsp ground red pepper**

1. In a large bowl, combine all ingredients except cooking spray; cover and set aside for at least 15 to 20 minutes (refrigerate if overnight). Coat a large skillet with cooking spray and place over medium heat until hot.
2. Shape mixture into 4 patties and place in hot skillet. Fry patties for 5 to 6 minutes on each side, remove, and let drain on paper towels. Transfer to serving platter and serve while hot.

....

Lean Meat Exchange 2	Total Carbohydrate . . . . 3 grams
Calories 113	Dietary Fiber . . . . 0 grams
Total Fat . . . . 6 grams	Sugars . . . . 0 grams
Saturated Fat . . . . 2 grams	Protein . . . . 11 grams
Calories from Fat 55	Sodium . . . . 69 milligrams
Cholesterol . . . . 30 milligrams	

WESTERN OMELET

2 servings/serving size: 1/2 omelet

Here's a good basic omelet recipe—experiment with your favorite vegetables.

- **1-1/2 tsp canola oil**
- **3 egg substitute equivalents**
- **1/4 cup minced lean ham**
- **2 Tbsp minced green pepper**
- **2 Tbsp minced onion**
- **Dash salt**
- **Fresh ground pepper**

1. In a medium nonstick skillet over medium-low heat, heat the oil.
2. In a small mixing bowl, beat eggs slightly and add remaining ingredients. Pour egg mixture into heated skillet.
3. When omelet begins to set, gently lift the edges of omelet with a spatula, and tilt skillet to allow uncooked portion to flow underneath. Continue cooking until eggs are firm, then transfer to serving platter.

....

Lean Meat Exchange	2	Total Carbohydrate	3 grams
Calories	96	Dietary Fiber	0 grams
Total Fat	4 grams	Sugars	2 grams
Saturated Fat	1 gram	Protein	11 grams
Calories from Fat	39	Sodium	379 milligrams
Cholesterol	8 milligrams		

DESSERTS

APPLE BREAD PUDDING

10 servings/serving size: 1/2 cup

*S*erve this pudding warm on those chilly winter nights!

- **5–6 cups cubed whole-wheat bread** (about 9 slices)
- **2 cups cubed apple** (Granny Smith work well)
- **4 cups skim milk**

- **4 egg substitute equivalents**
- **2 tsp vanilla**
- **2 tsp cinnamon**
- **1/4 cup fructose**
- **1/2 cup raisins**

1. Preheat the oven to 350 degrees. In a large baking dish, combine the bread and apples.
2. In a separate bowl, whisk together the milk, eggs, vanilla, cinnamon, and fructose. Add the raisins. Pour the milk mixture over the bread and let stand for 15 minutes so the bread can absorb some of the liquid.
3. Bake for 40 to 45 minutes until the bread pudding is set and firm. Cut into squares and serve warm with whipped topping or low-fat ice cream.

....

Starch Exchange 2
Calories 156
Total Fat . . . . 1 gram
   Saturated Fat . . . . 0 grams
   Calories from Fat 12
Cholesterol . . . . 2 milligrams

Total Carbohydrate . . . . 29 grams
   Dietary Fiber . . . . 3 grams
   Sugars . . . . 17 grams
Protein . . . . 8 grams
Sodium . . . . 218 milligrams

APPLE CRANBERRY CRISP

8 servings/serving size: 1/2 cup

*T*his is a great holiday dessert! It's good served with low-fat vanilla ice cream.

- ◆ 7 medium apples, cored and sliced
- ◆ 1 cup cranberries, chopped or left whole
- ◆ 2 Tbsp lemon juice
- ◆ 1 tsp cinnamon

- ◆ 1 tsp nutmeg
- ◆ 1/4 cup whole-wheat flour
- ◆ 1/2 cup rolled oats
- ◆ 2 Tbsp canola oil
- ◆ 2 Tbsp fructose
- ◆ 1 tsp vanilla

1. Preheat the oven to 325 degrees. Spray an 8x8x2-inch baking dish with nonstick cooking spray and layer the apples and cranberries in the dish.
2. Combine the lemon juice and spices in a small bowl; pour over the apples and cranberries.
3. Combine the flour, oats, oil, fructose, and vanilla and stir until the mixture looks like granola. Sprinkle over the apples and cranberries.
4. Bake the crisp uncovered for 20 minutes. Broil the top of the crisp for 2 minutes until the top is slightly browned, if desired.

....

Starch Exchange	1	Cholesterol	0 milligrams
Fruit Exchange	1	Total Carbohydrate	31 grams
Fat Exchange	1	Dietary Fiber	5 grams
Calories	161	Sugars	21 grams
Total Fat	4 grams	Protein	2 grams
Saturated Fat	0 grams	Sodium	1 milligram
Calories from Fat	40		

BANANA PINEAPPLE FREEZE

12 servings/serving size: 1/2 cup

*T*ry this dessert when you are in the mood for something cool and creamy without all the fat of ice cream. It's especially pretty served in wine or champagne glasses and topped with a sprig of mint.

- ◆ **2 cups mashed ripe bananas**
- ◆ **2 cups unsweetened orange juice**
- ◆ **2 Tbsp fresh lemon juice**
- ◆ **1 cup unsweetened crushed pineapple, undrained**
- ◆ **Ground cinnamon**

Combine all ingredients in a food processor, processing until smooth and creamy. Pour mixture into a 9x9x2-inch baking dish and freeze overnight or until firm. Serve chilled.

....

Fruit Exchange 1	Total Carbohydrate . . . . 14 grams
Calories 60	Dietary Fiber . . . . 1 gram
Total Fat . . . . 0 grams	Sugars . . . . 15 grams
Saturated Fat . . . . 0 grams	Protein . . . . 1 gram
Calories from Fat 0	Sodium . . . . 2 milligrams
Cholesterol . . . . 0 milligrams	

BANANAS FOSTER

8 servings/serving size: 1/2 cup ice cream
with 1/8 of the banana sauce

This is a light version of a classic, elegant favorite.

- 1/2 cup unsweetened
  pineapple juice
- 1/4 tsp cinnamon
- 3 large bananas
- 1 cup unsweetened sliced
  pineapple, drained

- 1/4 cup rum
- 1 qt low-calorie, low-fat ice
  cream

1. In a medium skillet, combine the pineapple juice and cinnamon.
2. Peel the bananas and slice in half crosswise; quarter each piece lengthwise.
3. Add the bananas and pineapple slices to juice mixture and cook over medium heat until bananas are soft, basting constantly with juice.
4. Place rum in a small, long-handled skillet and heat until warm. Ignite the rum with a long match and quickly pour over the fruit.
5. Arrange ice cream in a serving dish, spoon bananas over the ice cream, and serve immediately.

....

Starch Exchange	1-1/2	Cholesterol	5 milligrams
Fruit Exchange	1-1/2	Total Carbohydrate	43 grams
Calories	209	Dietary Fiber	3 grams
Total Fat	2 grams	Sugars	35 grams
Saturated Fat	2 grams	Protein	4 grams
Calories from Fat	22	Sodium	51 milligrams

BASIC CREPES

20 servings/serving size: two 6-inch crepes

*A*ny filling is great stuffed into these basic crepes, depending on whether you're serving hearty main entrees or spectacular desserts!

- ◆ **3 egg substitute equivalents**
- ◆ **1-1/3 cups flour**
- ◆ **1/2 tsp salt**
- ◆ **1-1/2 cups skim milk**
- ◆ **2 tsp canola oil**

1. Combine all ingredients in a food processor or blender. Process for 30 seconds, scraping down the sides of container. Continue to process until mixture is smooth; refrigerate for 1 hour.
2. Coat the bottom of a 6-inch crepe pan or small skillet with nonstick cooking spray. Place the pan over medium heat until hot but not smoking.
3. Pour 2 Tbsp of batter into the pan and quickly tilt it in all directions so that the batter covers the pan in a thin film. Cook for about 1 minute, lifting the edge of the crepe to test for doneness (the crepe is ready to be flipped when it can be shaken loose from the pan).
4. Flip the crepe and continue to cook for 30 seconds on the other side. (This side usually has brownish spots on it, so place the filling on this side.)
5. Stack the cooked crepes between layers of waxed paper to avoid sticking, and repeat the process with the remaining batter.

••

Starch Exchange	1	Total Carbohydrate	15 grams
Calories	89	Dietary Fiber	0 grams
Total Fat	1 gram	Sugars	2 grams
Saturated Fat	0 grams	Protein	4 grams
Calories from Fat	10	Sodium	150 milligrams
Cholesterol	1 milligram		

BASIC CREPES WITH FRUIT FILLING

10 servings/serving size: 2 filled crepes with topping

*F*or these fruity dessert crepes, select strawberries, blueberries, raspberries, or blackberries—or your own favorite fruit!

- **2 cups washed berries**
- **1 cup water**
- **2 tsp sugar substitute**
- **1-1/2 Tbsp cornstarch**
- **20 Basic Crepes** (see recipe, page 240)

- **Low-Calorie, Fat-Free Whipped Cream** (see recipe, page 255)

1. Combine all filling ingredients in a saucepan and bring to a boil. Lower heat until the mixture thickens.
2. Cool mixture slightly; place the fruit filling inside each of 20 crepes. Fold the crepe over to seal it. Top each crepe with 2 Tbsp of the whipped cream topping.

....

Starch Exchange	1-1/2	Total Carbohydrate	23 grams
Calories	136	Dietary Fiber	1 gram
Total Fat	1 gram	Sugars	8 grams
Saturated Fat	0 grams	Protein	8 grams
Calories from Fat	12	Sodium	205 milligrams
Cholesterol	2 milligrams		

BASIC PIE SHELL

8 servings/serving size: 1/8 shell

*H*ere's an easy, classic pie shell.

- **1/3 cup vegetable shortening, chilled**
- **3 Tbsp ice water**
- **1 cup flour, sifted**
- **1/4 tsp salt**

1. In a medium bowl, cut the shortening into the flour and salt until the mixture forms crumbs. Add the ice water, 1 Tbsp at a time, until you can form the mixture into a ball. Wrap the dough in plastic wrap and refrigerate for at least 1 hour.
2. Roll out the dough to fit a 9-inch pie pan. The pie shell can be filled at this point or pricked with a fork on the sides and bottom and prebaked for 10 minutes in a 450-degree oven. (Allow the prebaked pie shell to cool before filling.)

....

Starch Exchange 1	Cholesterol . . . . 0 milligrams
Fat Exchange 1-1/2	Total Carbohydrate . . . . 12 grams
Calories 145	Dietary Fiber . . . . 0 grams
Total Fat . . . . 10 grams	Sugars . . . . 0 grams
Saturated Fat . . . . 1 gram	Protein . . . . 2 grams
Calories from Fat 91	Sodium . . . . 67 milligrams

CARROT CAKE

16 servings/serving size: 1/16 plain cake

*A*pplesauce replaces some of the fat used in this dense, moist cake to produce a delicious, good-for-you taste!

- 1/2 cup canola oil
- 1/2 cup unsweetened applesauce
- 2 Tbsp sugar substitute
- 4 egg substitute equivalents
- 1/2 cup water
- 2 cups flour

- 1 tsp baking powder
- 1 tsp baking soda
- 2 tsp cinnamon
- 1/4 tsp nutmeg
- 1/2 tsp salt (optional)
- 1/2 cup chopped pecans
- 3 cups grated carrots

1. Preheat the oven to 350 degrees. In a large mixing bowl, beat together the oil, applesauce, sugar substitute, and eggs until well blended.
2. Add the water, flour, baking powder, baking soda, cinnamon, nutmeg, and salt and mix well.
3. Stir in the pecans and carrots. Coat a 3-quart tube pan with nonstick cooking spray. Pour in the batter and bake for 35 to 40 minutes or until a toothpick inserted in the cake comes out clean.
4. Let the cake cool 10 minutes in the pan, then invert cake and let cool completely. If you like, frost with Low-Fat Cream Cheese Frosting (see recipe, page 256).

....

Starch Exchange 1	Total Carbohydrate . . . . 15 grams
Fat Exchange 1-1/2	Dietary Fiber . . . . 1 gram
Calories 155	Sugars . . . . 2 grams
Total Fat . . . . 9 grams	Protein . . . . 3 grams
Saturated Fat . . . . 1 gram	Sodium . . . . 173 milligrams
Calories from Fat 83	w/o added salt . . . . . 106 milligrams
Cholesterol . . . . 0 milligrams	

CHERRY CHEESECAKE

8 servings/serving size: 1/8 pie

You can substitute blueberries or strawberries for the cherries in this creamy cheesecake if you like.

- ♦ **13 oz evaporated skimmed milk**
- ♦ **2 Tbsp cornstarch**
- ♦ **1 Tbsp liquid sugar substitute**
- ♦ **3 oz low-fat cream cheese, softened**
- ♦ **1/2 cup fresh lemon juice**

- ♦ **1 tsp vanilla extract**
- ♦ **1 prepared Crumb Pie shell** (see recipe, page 253)
- ♦ **12 oz unsweetened sour cherries, undrained**
- ♦ **2 Tbsp cornstarch**
- ♦ **1 Tbsp sugar substitute**

1. In a large saucepan over medium heat, heat the milk and cornstarch; stir constantly, but do not boil. Remove from heat, stir in the sugar substitute, and set aside to cool.

2. In a small bowl, beat the cream cheese until light and fluffy. Add to cool milk mixture; beat in lemon juice and vanilla. Pour mixture into prepared pie shell and refrigerate 2 to 3 hours or until firm.

3. To prepare the topping, drain the cherries over a saucepan so that only the liquid goes into the saucepan. Add cornstarch to the cherry liquid and simmer over medium heat until the mixture is thick and clear.

4. Stir in the cherries and sugar substitute, mixing thoroughly. Remove from heat and let cool. Spread topping over cream cheese and refrigerate until ready to serve.

....

Starch Exchange	2	Cholesterol	12 milligrams
Fat Exchange	1	Total Carbohydrate	30 grams
Calories	200	Dietary Fiber	1 gram
Total Fat	6 grams	Sugars	14 grams
Saturated Fat	2 grams	Protein	7 grams
Calories from Fat	55	Sodium	213 milligrams

CHERRY COBBLER

4 servings/serving size: 1/4 recipe

*Y*ou can find arrowroot powder in the spice aisle of the supermarket.

- ◆ 2 cups water-packed sour cherries
- ◆ 1/4 tsp fresh lemon juice
- ◆ 1/8 tsp almond extract
- ◆ 1/2 tsp arrowroot powder
- ◆ 1/2 cup flour, sifted
- ◆ 1/8 tsp salt (optional)

- ◆ 3/4 tsp baking powder
- ◆ 1 Tbsp low-calorie margarine
- ◆ 1 egg substitute equivalent
- ◆ 2 Tbsp skim milk
- ◆ 1/4 cup granulated sugar substitute

1. Preheat the oven to 425 degrees. Drain cherries, reserving 2/3 cup of liquid, and place the cherries in a shallow cake pan.
2. In a small mixing bowl, combine the lemon juice, almond extract, arrowroot and drained cherry liquid; mix well. Spoon over the cherries.
3. In a mixing bowl, combine the flour, salt, and baking powder. Mix thoroughly. Cut in margarine until coarse; add egg, milk, and sugar substitute, mixing well.
4. Spoon mixture over cherries and bake for 25 to 30 minutes or until crust is golden brown.

....

Starch Exchange 1	Total Carbohydrate . . . . 25 grams
Fruit Exchange 1	Dietary Fiber . . . . 2 grams
Calories 130	Sugars . . . . 12 grams
Total Fat . . . . 2 grams	Protein . . . . 4 grams
Saturated Fat . . . . 0 grams	Sodium . . . . 189 milligrams
Calories from Fat 15	w/o added salt . . . . . 120 milligrams
Cholesterol . . . . 0 milligrams	

CHERRY PIE

8 servings/serving size: 1/8 pie

This is a beautiful pie to make for company or Valentine's Day, with heart-shaped cutouts and warm red cherries!

- ◆ **32 oz water-packed sour cherries, undrained**
- ◆ **3 Tbsp cornstarch**
- ◆ **1/4 cup sugar substitute**
- ◆ **1/4 tsp almond extract**
- ◆ **Dash salt (optional)**
- ◆ **Red food coloring (optional)**
- ◆ **1 prepared Basic Pie Shell, unbaked** (see recipe, page 242—be sure to read step #3 in this recipe before rolling out the pie shell!)

1. Preheat the oven to 425 degrees. Drain cherries; reserve 1/2 cup of the juice.
2. In a large saucepan, combine the cherry juice, cornstarch, sugar substitute, almond extract, and salt. Let the mixture simmer over medium heat until slightly thickened. If you like, add a few drops of red food coloring to achieve a more intense color. Fold in the cherries and set aside.
3. Roll out the pie dough on a lightly floured surface into a circle larger than a 9-inch pie plate. Place the dough into the pie plate, securing it by pressing the edges with the tines of a fork. Cut away the excess dough and roll it out very thin. Cut out 8 heart-shaped designs with a cookie cutter; prick the sides and bottom of shell with a fork.
4. Pour cherry filling into pie shell, and arrange hearts evenly around the top. Bake for 40 to 50 minutes or until crust is lightly browned. If you like, serve with Low-Calorie, Fat-Free Whipped Cream (see recipe, page 255) or low-fat ice cream.

....

Starch Exchange	1/2	Cholesterol	0 milligrams
Fruit Exchange	1	Total Carbohydrate	25 grams
Fat Exchange	2	Dietary Fiber	1 gram
Calories	199	Sugars	10 grams
Total Fat	10 grams	Protein	2 grams
Saturated Fat	1 gram	Sodium	95 milligrams
Calories from Fat	92	w/o added salt	78 milligrams

CHERRY SOUFFLÉ

8 servings/serving size: 1/8 soufflé

*T*ry this soufflé when you want something different from a traditional pie.

- ◆ 3/4 cup water
- ◆ 1 pkg. unflavored gelatin
- ◆ 2 cups water-packed sour cherries, drained and chopped
- ◆ 1 Tbsp fresh lemon juice

- ◆ 2 Tbsp sugar substitute
- ◆ 3 large egg whites
- ◆ 2 cups prepared Low-Calorie, Fat-Free Whipped Cream (see recipe, page 255)

1. In a medium saucepan, combine the water and gelatin; allow to soften for 10 to 15 minutes. Add 1 cup of the cherries, lemon juice, and sugar substitute; bring to a boil.
2. Remove from heat and let cool; refrigerate until thick and syrupy.
3. Fold in remaining cherries, beaten egg whites, and whipped cream. Spoon into a soufflé dish and refrigerate until set.

Starch Exchange 1
Calories 68
Total Fat . . . . 0 grams
  Saturated Fat . . . . 0 grams
  Calories from Fat 0
Cholesterol . . . . 2 milligrams

Total Carbohydrate . . . . 11 grams
  Dietary Fiber . . . . 1 gram
  Sugars . . . . 10 grams
Protein . . . . 6 grams
Sodium . . . . 68 milligrams

CHOCOLATE CHIP COOKIES

10 servings/serving size: 3 cookies

This version of chocolate chip cookies has a delicious cake-like texture.

- 1/4 cup low-calorie margarine
- 1 Tbsp granulated fructose
- 1 egg substitute equivalent
- 3 Tbsp water
- 1 tsp vanilla
- 3/4 cup flour
- 1/4 tsp baking soda
- 1/4 tsp salt
- 1/2 cup semisweet chocolate chips

1. Preheat the oven to 375 degrees. In a medium bowl, cream the margarine and the fructose. Beat in the egg, water, and vanilla; mix thoroughly.
2. In a sifter, combine the flour, baking soda, and salt. Sift the dry ingredients into the creamed mixture and mix well. Stir in the chocolate chips.
3. Lightly spray cookie sheets with nonstick cooking spray. Drop teaspoonfuls of dough onto cookie sheets and bake for 8 to 10 minutes. Remove the cookies from the oven and cool them on racks.

....

Starch Exchange	....	1
Fat Exchange	....	1/2
Calories	....	101
Total Fat	....	5 grams
Saturated Fat	....	2 grams
Calories from Fat	....	44

Cholesterol	....	0 milligrams
Total Carbohydrate	....	14 grams
Dietary Fiber	....	1 gram
Sugars	....	6 grams
Protein	....	2 grams
Sodium	....	119 milligrams

CHOCOLATE CUPCAKES

12 servings/serving size: 1 cupcake

A *healthier version of everyone's favorite! Try frosting these with Low-Fat Cream Cheese Frosting (see recipe, page 256).*

- 2 Tbsp low-calorie margarine
- 2 Tbsp canola oil
- 1/4 cup fructose
- 1 egg substitute equivalent
- 1 tsp vanilla
- 1/2 cup skim milk

- 1-1/4 cups flour
- 1/4 cup ground walnuts
- 6 Tbsp cocoa powder
- 2 tsp baking powder
- 1/4 tsp baking soda

1. Preheat the oven to 375 degrees. Beat the margarine with the oil until creamy. Add the fructose, then egg, vanilla, and milk.
2. In a separate bowl, combine the flour, walnuts, cocoa, baking powder, and baking soda. Add to the creamed mixture and mix until smooth.
3. Spoon the batter into paper-lined muffin tins and bake for 20 minutes. Remove from the oven and let cool.

....

Starch Exchange 1	Cholesterol .... 0 milligrams
Fat Exchange 1	Total Carbohydrate .... 15 grams
Calories 113	Dietary Fiber .... 1 gram
Total Fat .... 5 grams	Sugars .... 4 grams
Saturated Fat .... 1 gram	Protein .... 3 grams
Calories from Fat 47	Sodium .... 94 milligrams

CHOCOLATE RUM PIE

8 servings/serving size: 1/8 pie

*J*ust a hint of rum complements the chocolate in this elegant dessert.

- 1 pkg. unflavored gelatin
- 1 cup skim milk
- 2 eggs, separated
- 2 Tbsp granulated sugar substitute
- Dash salt (optional)
- 1/4 cup cocoa
- 1 tsp rum extract
- 1 Tbsp liquid sugar substitute
- 2 cups low-calorie commercial whipped topping
- 1 Basic Pie shell, baked (see recipe, page 242)

1. In a large saucepan, combine gelatin, milk, egg yolks, granulated sugar substitute, salt, and cocoa. Cook over medium heat until completely blended and slightly thickened.
2. Remove from heat, stir in the rum extract and refrigerate the mixture until partially set.
3. In a small bowl, beat egg whites with liquid sugar substitute until stiff peaks form. Fold into cooled chocolate mixture.
4. Layer the chocolate mixture and whipped topping in the pie shell, ending with whipped topping. Refrigerate for 2 to 3 hours or until firm.

....

Starch Exchange	1-1/2	Total Carbohydrate	19 grams
Fat Exchange	2	Dietary Fiber	1 gram
Calories	216	Sugars	6 grams
Total Fat	13 grams	Protein	5 grams
Saturated Fat	2 grams	Sodium	138 milligrams
Calories from Fat	113	w/o added salt	120 milligrams
Cholesterol	54 milligrams		

CREAM CHEESE COOKIES

15 servings/serving size: 2 cookies

You can freeze the rolled dough for these cookies (after step #2), pull it out when you need it, and make warm cookies fast for holidays or special occasions!

- ◆ 1/4 cup vegetable shortening
- ◆ 1/4 cup low-fat cream cheese, softened
- ◆ 1 Tbsp fructose
- ◆ 1 egg substitute equivalent
- ◆ 1 Tbsp water
- ◆ 1 cup flour
- ◆ 1/2 tsp baking powder
- ◆ Dash salt (optional)

1. In a food processor, combine shortening, cream cheese, and fructose; mix until creamy in texture. Add the egg substitute and water; mix thoroughly.
2. Sift flour, baking powder, and salt (if desired) together and add to creamed mixture; blend well. Shape into a roll about 1-1/2 inches in diameter and refrigerate overnight.
3. Cut into 1-1/2–inch slices and place on ungreased cookie sheets. Bake at 350 degrees for 8 to 10 minutes or until the tops are golden brown. Remove cookies from the oven, and let them cool on racks.

• •

Starch Exchange	1/2	Total Carbohydrate	7 grams
Fat Exchange	1	Dietary Fiber	0 grams
Calories	78	Sugars	1 gram
Total Fat	5 grams	Protein	2 grams
Saturated Fat	1 gram	Sodium	37 milligrams
Calories from Fat	43	w/o added salt	6 milligrams
Cholesterol	2 milligrams		

CREPES SUZETTE

8 servings/serving size: 2 crepes

*N*ow *you can make this classic French recipe—always dramatic to serve!*

- **2 cups unsweetened orange juice**
- **2 Tbsp cornstarch**
- **1 Tbsp orange rind**
- **2 medium oranges, peeled and sectioned**
- **16 Basic Crepes** (see recipe, page 240)
- **1/4 cup Grand Marnier**

1. In a large skillet, combine the orange juice, cornstarch, and orange rind. Bring the mixture to a boil over medium heat. Boil for 1 to 2 minutes, stirring occasionally.
2. Add the orange sections and remove from heat. Allow the mixture to cool slightly.
3. Dip both sides of the crepes in sauce; fold in quarters. Arrange crepes in the skillet in the remaining sauce; heat completely over low heat.
4. Heat (do not boil!) Grand Marnier in a saucepan over medium heat, then ignite it with a long match and pour over the crepes. Serve when the flame subsides.

....

Starch Exchange 2	Total Carbohydrate .... 31 grams
Calories 156	Dietary Fiber .... 1 gram
Total Fat .... 1 gram	Sugars .... 16 grams
Saturated Fat .... 0 grams	Protein .... 5 grams
Calories from Fat 11	Sodium .... 151 milligrams
Cholesterol .... 1 milligram	

CRUMB PIE SHELL

8 servings/serving size: 1/8 shell

You can use this basic pie shell with almost any filling!

- ◆ **1-1/4 cups finely crumbled Zwieback crackers**
- ◆ **3 Tbsp low-calorie margarine, melted**
- ◆ **1 Tbsp water**
- ◆ **1/8 tsp cinnamon**

1. In a medium mixing bowl, combine the cracker crumbs, margarine, water and cinnamon, mixing thoroughly.
2. Spread the mixture evenly into a 10-inch pie pan. Press the mixture firmly onto the sides and bottom of the pan.
3. Bake at 325 degrees for 8 to 10 minutes, or refrigerate after baking until ready to use.

....

Starch/Bread Exchange 1	Cholesterol . . . . 4 milligrams
Fat Exchange 1/2	Total Carbohydrate . . . . 15 grams
Calories 104	Dietary Fiber . . . . 1 gram
Total Fat . . . . 4 grams	Sugars . . . . 3 grams
Saturated Fat . . . . 1 gram	Protein . . . . 2 grams
Calories from Fat 37	Sodium . . . . 80 milligrams

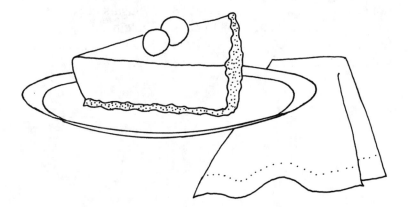

FRESH APPLE PIE

8 servings/serving size: 1/8 pie

You can substitute peaches or berries for the apples in this delicious homemade pie.

- **10 medium baking apples** (Rome work well), **peeled, cored, and sliced**
- **2 tsp fresh lemon juice**
- **1 prepared Basic Pie Shell, unbaked** (see recipe, page 242)
- **2 Tbsp granulated sugar substitute**
- **1 Tbsp flour**
- **1 tsp ground cinnamon**
- **1/2 tsp ground nutmeg**

1. Preheat the oven to 425 degrees. Place the sliced apples in a large bowl, sprinkle with lemon juice, and toss to coat. Arrange the apples in the pie shell.

2. In a small bowl, combine the sugar substitute, flour, cinnamon and nutmeg; mix well. Sprinkle the mixture over the apples and bake the pie for 35 to 40 minutes or until the crust is golden brown. Remove from the oven and cool slightly before serving.

....

Starch Exchange	1	Cholesterol .... 0 milligrams
Fruit Exchange	2	Total Carbohydrate .... 43 grams
Fat Exchange	1-1/2	Dietary Fiber .... 6 grams
Calories	268	Sugars .... 26 grams
Total Fat	11 grams	Protein .... 2 grams
Saturated Fat	1 gram	Sodium .... 69 milligrams
Calories from Fat	98	

LOW-CALORIE, FAT-FREE WHIPPED CREAM

8 servings/serving size: 2 Tbsp

Use this delicious whipped cream topping on fruit, pies, or cakes.

- ◆ 2 Tbsp water
- ◆ 1 tsp unflavored gelatin
- ◆ 1/2 cup nonfat powdered milk
- ◆ 1 tsp vanilla extract
- ◆ 1 cup ice water
- ◆ 1/2 tsp liquid sugar substitute

1. In a small skillet, add the water; sprinkle gelatin on top.
2. After the gelatin has soaked in, stir over low heat until clear; cool. In a large mixing bowl, combine the milk, vanilla, ice water, and sugar substitute; mix well.
3. Add the gelatin mixture and whip until fluffy with a wire whisk or electric beaters. Refrigerate until ready to use.

....

Free Food*

Calories	16
Total Fat	0 grams
Saturated Fat	0 grams
Calories from Fat	0
Cholesterol	1 milligram

Total Carbohydrate	2 grams
Dietary Fiber	0 grams
Sugars	2 grams
Protein	2 grams
Sodium	25 milligrams

*Remember that only 2 Tbsp or less is a Free Food!

LOW-FAT CREAM CHEESE FROSTING

48 servings/serving size: 2 Tbsp

This is a delicious, low-fat version of an old favorite!

- 3 cups skim-milk ricotta cheese
- 1-1/3 cups plain nonfat yogurt, strained overnight in cheesecloth over a bowl set in the refrigerator

- 2 cups low-fat cottage cheese
- 1/3 cup fructose
- 3 Tbsp evaporated skim milk

Combine all the ingredients in a large bowl; beat well with electric beaters until slightly stiff. Place in a covered container and refrigerate until ready to use (this frosting can be refrigerated for up to 1 week).

Skim Milk Exchange 1/2
Calories 38
Total Fat . . . . 1 gram
   Saturated Fat . . . . 1 gram
   Calories from Fat 13
Cholesterol . . . . 6 milligrams

Total Carbohydrate . . . . 3 grams
   Dietary Fiber . . . . 0 grams
   Sugars . . . . 2 grams
Protein . . . . 3 grams
Sodium . . . . 63 milligrams

OATMEAL RAISIN COOKIES

24 servings/serving size: 2 cookies

Whole-wheat flour and oats add fiber to these tasty cookies.

- 3 cups rolled oats
- 1 cup whole-wheat flour
- 1 tsp baking soda
- 2 tsp cinnamon
- 1/2 cup raisins
- 1/4 cup unsweetened applesauce

- 1/4 cup fructose
- 2 egg substitute equivalents
- 1/2 cup plain nonfat yogurt
- 1 tsp vanilla

1. Preheat the oven to 350 degrees. Combine the oats, flour, baking soda, cinnamon, and raisins.
2. Beat the applesauce, fructose, eggs, yogurt, and vanilla in a large bowl until creamy. Slowly add the dry ingredients and mix together.
3. Spray cookie sheets with nonstick cooking spray and drop by teaspoonfuls onto the cookie sheets. Bake for 12 to 15 minutes; transfer to racks and cool.

....

Starch Exchange 1
Calories 76
Total Fat . . . . 1 gram
   Saturated Fat . . . . 0 grams
   Calories from Fat 7
Cholesterol . . . . 0 milligrams

Total Carbohydrate . . . . 15 grams
   Dietary Fiber . . . . 2 grams
   Sugars . . . . 4 grams
Protein . . . . 3 grams
Sodium . . . . 46 milligrams

PEACH CRUMB COBBLER

4 servings/serving size: 1/2 cup

If you like, you can substitute pears, apples, or berries for the peaches in this tasty cobbler.

- **2 cups fresh peaches, sliced**
- **1/3 cup graham cracker crumbs**
- **1/2 tsp ground cinnamon**
- **1/4 tsp nutmeg**
- **2 tsp low-calorie margarine**

1. Preheat the oven to 350 degrees. Place the sliced peaches in the bottom of an 8x8x2-inch baking pan. In a small mixing bowl, combine the graham cracker crumbs, cinnamon, and nutmeg; mix well.
2. Gradually blend in margarine and sprinkle mixture over peaches. Bake uncovered for 25 to 30 minutes. Remove from oven and let cool slightly before serving.

....

Fruit Exchange 1	Total Carbohydrate . . . . 15 grams
Calories 74	Dietary Fiber . . . . 2 grams
Total Fat . . . . 2 grams	Sugars . . . . 9 grams
Saturated Fat . . . . 0 grams	Protein . . . . 1 gram
Calories from Fat 15	Sodium . . . . 57 milligrams
Cholesterol . . . . 0 milligrams	

PEACH SHORTCAKE

8 servings/serving size: 1/2 cup

This is a perfect summer dessert—fresh peaches over a tender cake crust.

- **2 cups sliced fresh peaches**
- **1-1/2 Tbsp plus 1 tsp sugar substitute**
- **1/2 tsp almond extract**
- **1/2 tsp cinnamon**
- **1 cup flour**
- **2 tsp baking powder**
- **Dash salt (optional)**
- **2 Tbsp canola oil**
- **1 egg substitute equivalent**
- **1/4 cup skim milk**

1. Preheat the oven to 400 degrees. Lightly spray an 8x8x2-inch baking pan with nonstick cooking spray. Arrange the peaches in the bottom of the dish.
2. Mix together 1 tsp sugar substitute, almond extract, and cinnamon; sprinkle over the peaches and set aside. In a medium mixing bowl, combine the flour, baking powder, salt, and 1-1/2 Tbsp sugar substitute; mix well.
3. Add the oil, egg, and milk to the dry ingredients; mix until smooth. Spread evenly over the peaches and bake for 25 to 30 minutes or until the top is golden brown. Remove from oven, invert onto a serving plate, and serve.

Starch Exchange	1	Total Carbohydrate	18 grams
Fruit Exchange	1/2	Dietary Fiber	1 gram
Calories	114	Sugars	5 grams
Total Fat	4 grams	Protein	3 grams
Saturated Fat	0 grams	Sodium	110 milligrams
Calories from Fat	33	w/o added salt	94 milligrams
Cholesterol	0 milligrams		

PEANUT BUTTER COOKIES

14 servings/serving size: 3 cookies

*N*ote that these cookies require overnight refrigeration before baking!

- 1/4 cup low-calorie margarine
- 1/4 cup creamy peanut butter
- 2 Tbsp brown sugar substitute
- 1 egg substitute equivalent
- 1/4 cup water

- 1 tsp vanilla
- 1-1/2 cups flour
- 1 tsp baking soda
- 1/2 tsp baking powder

1. In a food processor or by hand, cream together the margarine, peanut butter, and sugar substitute. Add the egg, water, and vanilla and continue to mix until well blended.
2. Combine the flour, baking soda, and baking powder in a sifter; sift dry ingredients into creamed mixture and mix until completely blended. Refrigerate overnight.
3. Lightly spray cookie sheets with nonstick cooking spray. Drop teaspoonfuls onto cookie sheets and press with the tines of a fork to flatten each cookie. Bake the cookies at 375 degrees for 12 to 15 minutes, remove from the oven, and let them cool on racks.

....

Starch Exchange	. . . .	1
Fat Exchange	. . . .	1/2
Calories	. . . .	100
Total Fat	. . . .	4 grams
Saturated Fat	. . . .	1 gram
Calories from Fat	. . . .	36

Cholesterol	. . . .	0 milligrams
Total Carbohydrate	. . . .	13 grams
Dietary Fiber	. . . .	1 gram
Sugars	. . . .	3 grams
Protein	. . . .	3 grams
Sodium	. . . .	123 milligrams

PINEAPPLE PEAR MEDLEY

12 servings/serving size: 1/2 cup

Cooking the fruit juices and then allowing the dish to cool in the refrigerator creates a unique, refreshing flavor.

- ◆ 1 large orange
- ◆ 15-oz can unsweetened pineapple chunks, undrained
- ◆ 32 oz unsweetened pear halves, drained
- ◆ 16-oz can unsweetened apricot halves, drained
- ◆ 6 whole cloves
- ◆ 2 cinnamon sticks

1. Peel the orange and reserve the rind. Divide the orange into sections and remove the membrane.
2. Drain the pineapple, reserve the juice, and set aside. In a large bowl, combine the orange sections, pineapple, pears, and apricots. Toss and set aside.
3. In a small saucepan over medium heat, combine orange rind, pineapple juice, cloves, and cinnamon. Let simmer for 5 to 10 minutes, then strain the juices and pour over the fruit.
4. Cover and refrigerate for at least 2–3 hours. Toss before serving.

....

Fruit Exchange 1
Calories 50
Total Fat . . . . 0 grams
  Saturated Fat . . . . 0 grams
  Calories from Fat 0
Cholesterol . . . . 0 milligrams
Total Carbohydrate . . . . 13 grams
  Dietary Fiber . . . . 3 grams
  Sugars . . . . 10 grams
Protein . . . . 1 gram
Sodium . . . . 3 milligrams

PUMPKIN MOUSSE

4 servings/serving size: 1/2 cup

*T*his *is a perfect fall addition to your Thanksgiving buffet table.*

- 1 pkg. unflavored gelatin
- 1/2 cup water
- 2/3 cup instant nonfat milk powder
- 1/2 cup mashed pumpkin
- 2 Tbsp sugar substitute
- 1/2 tsp vanilla extract
- 1 tsp pumpkin pie spice
- 6 ice cubes

1. Combine the gelatin and water in a small saucepan and let stand for 1–2 minutes. Place over medium heat, stirring constantly, for 1 to 2 minutes or until gelatin is dissolved.
2. Combine the gelatin, milk, pumpkin, sugar substitute, vanilla, and pumpkin pie spice in blender or food processor; process until very smooth. Add ice cubes to the mixture, one at a time, blending thoroughly after each addition.
3. Pour into 4 parfait glasses or dessert dishes, cover, and refrigerate for 2 to 3 hours before serving. Top with low-calorie whipped cream if desired (see recipe, page 255).

....

Starch Exchange 1/2	Total Carbohydrate . . . . 9 grams
Calories 61	Dietary Fiber . . . . 1 gram
Total Fat . . . . 0 grams	Sugars . . . . 8 grams
Saturated Fat . . . . 0 grams	Protein . . . . 6 grams
Calories from Fat 0	Sodium . . . . 72 milligrams
Cholesterol . . . . 2 milligrams	

SPONGE CAKE

12 servings/serving size: 1/12 plain cake

*T*ry *topping this light sponge cake with fresh fruit and Low-Calorie, Fat-Free Whipped Cream (see recipe, page 255), and you'll have a delicious summer dessert!*

- ◆ **4 large eggs, separated**
- ◆ **3 Tbsp granulated sugar substitute**
- ◆ **1/2 cup hot water**
- ◆ **1-1/2 tsp vanilla extract**
- ◆ **1-1/2 cups cake flour, sifted**
- ◆ **1/4 tsp salt**
- ◆ **1/4 tsp baking powder**

1. Preheat the oven to 325 degrees. In a medium bowl, beat egg yolks and sugar substitute until thick and lemon-colored. Add the hot water and vanilla and continue beating for 3 more minutes.
2. In a sifter, combine flour, salt, and baking powder; add to the egg yolk mixture.
3. Beat the egg whites until stiff and fold into egg yolk mixture. Spoon batter into an ungreased 9-inch tube pan and bake for 50 to 60 minutes or until a toothpick inserted comes out clean.
4. Remove the cake from the oven and invert it onto a plate. Allow the cake to sit inverted in its pan for at least 1 hour. Remove the pan and let cake cool completely.

Starch Exchange	1	Total Carbohydrate .... 11 grams
Calories	76	Dietary Fiber .... 0 grams
Total Fat	2 grams	Sugars .... 1 gram
Saturated Fat	1 gram	Protein .... 3 grams
Calories from Fat	16	Sodium .... 74 milligrams
Cholesterol	71 milligrams	

STRAWBERRIES ROMANOFF

4 servings/serving size: 1 cup

*T*he low-fat versions of ice cream and whipped cream make this recipe healthy and delicious!

- **2 cups fresh strawberries, hulled**
- **1 cup low-fat vanilla ice cream**
- **1 Tbsp orange marmalade**

- **1 tsp rum extract**
- **1/2 cup Low-Calorie Fat-Free Whipped Cream** (see recipe, page 255)

1. Divide strawberries evenly between 4 serving dishes and refrigerate.
2. Just before serving, fold ice cream, orange marmalade, rum extract, and whipped cream together in a medium bowl. Spoon evenly over chilled strawberries and serve.

....

Fruit Exchange	1	Total Carbohydrate	17 grams
Calories	92	Dietary Fiber	1 gram
Total Fat	1 gram	Sugars	16 grams
Saturated Fat	1 gram	Protein	4 grams
Calories from Fat	11	Sodium	52 milligrams
Cholesterol	3 milligrams		

STRAWBERRIES WITH STRAWBERRY SAUCE

6 servings/serving size: 1/2 cup

Strawberry fans will love this easy, fast dessert!

- ◆ **4 cups fresh strawberries, washed and stemmed**
- ◆ **1 tsp sugar substitute**
- ◆ **2 Tbsp fresh orange juice**
- ◆ **1/2 cup fresh blueberries for topping**

1. Divide 2 cups of strawberries among 6 dessert dishes.
2. Puree the remaining 2 cups of strawberries in a blender with the sugar substitute and orange juice. Pour the sauce evenly over the dessert cups. Top each dessert cup with blueberries.

Fruit Exchange 1/2
Calories 41
Total Fat . . . . 0 grams
   Saturated Fat . . . . 0 grams
   Calories from Fat 0
Cholesterol . . . . 0 milligrams

Total Carbohydrate . . . . 10 grams
   Dietary Fiber . . . . 3 grams
   Sugars . . . . 6 grams
Protein . . . . 1 gram
Sodium . . . . 2 milligrams

WALNUT MACAROONS

21 servings/serving size: 2 cookies

Note that you'll need to refrigerate this cookie dough overnight.

- **2 cups quick-cooking oats**
- **2 Tbsp sugar substitute**
- **1/4 tsp salt (optional)**
- **2 tsp vanilla**

- **1/2 cup canola oil**
- **1 egg substitute equivalent, beaten**
- **1/2 cup finely chopped walnuts**

1. In a medium bowl, combine the oats, sugar substitute, salt, vanilla, and oil; mix thoroughly. Cover and refrigerate overnight. Add eggs and walnuts to mixture; blend thoroughly.
2. Pack cookie mixture into a teaspoon, level, and push out onto ungreased cookie sheets. Bake at 350 degrees for 15 minutes or until tops are golden brown. Transfer cookies to racks and cool.

....

Starch Exchange 1/2
Fat Exchange 1
Calories 84
Total Fat .... 7 grams
   Saturated Fat .... 1 gram
   Calories from Fat 59
Cholesterol .... 0 milligrams

Total Carbohydrate .... 5 grams
   Dietary Fiber .... 1 gram
   Sugars .... 0 grams
Protein .... 2 grams
Sodium .... 31 milligrams
   w/o added salt .... 4 milligrams

INDEX

COOKBOOKS & MEAL PLANNERS

NEW!
Memorable Menus Made Easy
Make homemade meals special occasions for family or friends—without extra effort, time, cost or bother. Here are 50 complete menus, every one following ADA guidelines for fat, carbohydrates, and sugar. Also offers timesaving tips for shopping and total preparation time, pantry and shopping lists, and a "step-by-step countdown" of which steps to do when.
Softcover. #4619-01
Nonmember: $19.95/ADA Member: $17.95

NEW!
The Diabetes Carbohydrate and Fat Gram Guide
Calories are important, but knowing the fat and carbohydrate content of the foods you eat is the key to eating right. Registered dietitian Lea Ann Holzmeister shows you how to count carbohydrate and fat grams and exchanges, and why it's important. Charts list foods, serving sizes, and nutrient data for hundreds of products.
Softcover. #4708-01
Nonmember: $11.95/ADA Member: $9.95

NEW!
Brand-Name Diabetic Meals in Minutes
Save time cooking with these popular taste-tested recipes from the kitchens of Campbell Soup, Kraft Foods, Weetabix, Dean Foods, Eskimo Pie, and Equal. Features more than 200 recipes from appetizers to desserts that will help make your meals tastier and your life easier. Nutrient information included.
Softcover. #4620-01
Nonmember: $12.95/ADA Member: $10.95

NEW!
How to Cook for People with Diabetes
Finally, a collection of reader favorites from the delicious, nutritious recipes featured every month in *Diabetes Forecast*. But you get more than pizza, chicken, unique holiday foods, vegetarian recipes and more—you also get nutrient analysis and exchanges for each recipe.
Softcover. #4616-01
Nonmember: $11.95/ADA Member: $9.95

NEW!
Magic Menus for People with Diabetes
Now you can plan all your meals from more than 50 breakfasts, 50 lunches, 75 dinners, and 30 snacks. Like magic, this book figures calories and exchanges for you automatically. The day's calories will still equal 1,300, 1,500, or 1,800, depending on your needs. Thousands of combinations are possible.
Softcover. #4707-01
Nonmember: $14.95/ADA Member: $12.95

NEW!
World-Class Diabetic Cooking
Travel around the world at every meal with this collection of 200 exciting new low-fat, low-calorie recipes. Features recipes from Thailand, Italy, Greece, Spain, China, Japan, Africa, Mexico, Germany, and more. Appetizers, soups, salads, pastas, meats, breads, and desserts are highlighted.
Softcover. #4617-01
Nonmember: $12.95/ADA Member: $10.95

NEW!
Southern-Style Diabetic Cooking
This cookbook takes traditional Southern dishes and turns them into great-tasting recipes you'll come back to again and again. Features more than 100 recipes including appetizers, main dishes, and desserts; complete nutrient analysis with each recipe; and suggestions for modifying recipes to meet individual nutritional needs.
Softcover. #4615-01
Nonmember: $11.95/ADA Member: $9.95

Flavorful Seasons Cookbook
Warm up your winter with recipes for the holidays, welcome spring with fresh vegetables, and cool off those hot summer days with more recipes for the Fourth of July. Here are more than 400 unforgettable choices that combine great taste with all the good-for-you benefits of a well-balanced meal. Find Cornish Game Hens, Orange Sea Bass, Ginger Bread Pudding, many others.
Softcover. #4613-01
Nonmember: $16.95/ADA Member: $14.95

Diabetic Meals In 30 Minutes—Or Less!
Put an end to bland, time-consuming meals with more than 140 fast, flavorful recipes. Complete nutrition information accompanies every recipe. A number of "quick tips" will have you out of the kitchen and into the dining room even faster! Look for Salsa Salad, Oven-Baked Parmesan Zucchini, Roasted Red Pepper Soup, Layered Vanilla Parfait, and more.
Softcover. #4614-01
Nonmember: $11.95/ADA Member: $9.95

Diabetes Meal Planning Made Easy
Learn quick and easy ways to eat more starches, fruits, vegetables, and milk; make changes in your eating habits to reach your goals; and understand how to use the Nutrition Facts on food labels. You'll also master the intricacies of each food group in the new Diabetes Food Pyramid.
Softcover. #4706-01
Nonmember: $14.95/ADA Member: $12.95

Month of Meals
When celebrations begin, go ahead—dig in! Includes a Special Occasion section that offers tips for brunches, holidays, and restaurants to give you delicious dining options anytime, anywhere. Menu choices include Chicken Cacciatore, Oven Fried Fish, Sloppy Joes, Crab Cakes, and many others.
Spiral-bound. #4707-01
Nonmember: $14.95/ADA Member: $12.95

Month of Meals 2
Automatic menu planning goes ethnic! Tips and meal suggestions for Mexican, Italian, and Chinese restaurants are featured. Quick-to-fix and ethnic recipes are also included. Find Beef Burritos, Chop Suey, Veal Piccata, Stuffed Peppers, and others. Spiral-bound. #4702-01
Nonmember: $14.95/ADA Member: $12.95

Month of Meals 3
Enjoy fast food without guilt! Make delicious choices at McDonald's, Wendy's, Taco Bell, and other fast food restaurants. Special sections offer valuable tips on reading labels, preparing meals for picnics, and meal planning when you're ill. Spiral-bound. #4703-01
Nonmember: $14.95/ADA Member: $12.95

Month of Meals 4
Meat and potatoes menu planning! Enjoy old-time family favorites like Meatloaf and Pot Roast, Crispy Fried Chicken, Beef Stroganoff, and many others. Hints for turning family-size meals into delicious left-overs will keep generous portions from going to waste. Meal plans for one or two people are also featured. Spiral-bound. #4704-01
Nonmember: $14.95/ADA Member: $12.95

Month of Meals 5
Meatless meals picked fresh from the garden. Choose from a garden of fresh vegetarian selections like Eggplant Italian, Stuffed Zucchini, Cucumbers with Dill Dressing, Vegetable Lasagna, and many others. Plus, you'll reap all the health benefits of a vegetarian diet. Spiral-bound. #4705-01
Nonmember: $14.95/ADA Member: $12.95

To order, call 800-232-6733 and mention code CK1297QE.

To join the ADA, call 800-806-7801.

ABOUT THE AMERICAN DIABETES ASSOCIATION

The American Diabetes Association is the nation's leading voluntary health organization supporting diabetes research, information, and advocacy. Founded in 1940, the Association provides services to communities across the country. Its mission is to prevent and cure diabetes and to improve the lives of all people affected by diabetes.

For more than 50 years, the American Diabetes Association has been the leading publisher of comprehensive diabetes information for people with diabetes and the health care professionals who treat them. Its huge library of practical and authoritative books for people with diabetes covers every aspect of self care—cooking and nutrition, fitness, weight control, medications, complications, emotional issues, and general self care. The Association also publishes books and medical treatment guides for physicians and other health care professionals.

Membership in the Association is available to health care professionals and people with diabetes and includes subscriptions to one or more of the Association's periodicals. People with diabetes receive *Diabetes Forecast*, the nation's leading health and wellness magazine for people with diabetes. Health care professionals receive one or more of the Association's five scientific and medical journals.

For more information, please call toll-free:

Questions about diabetes:	1-800-DIABETES
Membership, people with diabetes:	1-800-806-7801
Membership, health professionals:	1-800-232-3472
Free catalog of ADA books:	1-800-232-6733
Visit us on the Web:	www.diabetes.org
Visit us at our Web bookstore:	www.diabetes.store